Praise for *In*

"Unlike any other publisher – actual aut[...] happening in industry." – Paul A. Sellers, [...] and Remarketing, Hyundai Motor America

"What C-Level executives read to keep their edge and make pivotal business decisions. Timeless classics for indispensable knowledge." – Richard Costello, Manager-Corporate Marketing Communication, General Electric

"Want to know what the real leaders are thinking about now? It's in here." – Carl Ledbetter, SVP & CTO, Novell, Inc.

"Aspatore has tapped into a gold mine of knowledge and expertise ignored by other publishing houses." – Jack Barsky, Managing Director, Information Technology & Chief Information Officer, ConEdison *Solutions*

"Priceless wisdom from experts at applying technology in support of business objectives." – Frank Campagnoni, CTO, GE Global Exchange Services

"Aspatore publishes the answers to every business person's questions." – Al Cotton, Director, Nypro Corporate Image, Nypro Inc

"Everything good books should be - honest, informative, inspiring, and incredibly well-written." – Patti D. Hill, President, BlabberMouth PR

"Answers questions that others don't even begin to ask." – Bart Stuck, Managing Director, Signal Lake LLC

"Unique insights into the way the experts think and the lessons they've learned from experience." – MT Rainey, Co-CEO, Young & Rubicam/Rainey Kelly Campbell Roalfe

"Must have information for business executives." – Alex Wilmerding, Principal, Boston Capital Ventures

"Reading about real-world strategies from real working people beats the typical business book hands down." – Andrew Ceccon, Chief Marketing Officer, OnlineBenefits, Inc.

"Books of this publisher are syntheses of actual experiences of real-life, hands-on, front-line leaders--no academic or theoretical nonsense here. Comprehensive, tightly organized, yet nonetheless motivational!" – Lac V. Tran, Sr. Vice President, CIO and Associate Dean Rush University Medical Center

"Aspatore is unlike other publishers…books feature cutting-edge information provided by top executives working on the front-line of an industry." – Debra Reisenthel, President and CEO, Novasys Medical, Inc

www.Aspatore.com

Aspatore Books is the largest and most exclusive publisher of C-level executives (CEO, CFO, CTO, CMO, partner) from the world's most respected companies and law firms. Aspatore annually publishes a select group of C-level executives from the Global 1,000, top 250 law firms (partners and chairs), and other leading companies of all sizes. C-Level Business Intelligence™, as conceptualized and developed by Aspatore Books, provides professionals of all levels with proven business intelligence from industry insiders—direct and unfiltered insight from those who know it best—as opposed to third-party accounts offered by unknown authors and analysts. Aspatore Books is committed to publishing an innovative line of business and legal books, those which lay forth principles and offer insights that, when employed, can have a direct financial impact on the reader's business objectives, whatever they may be. In essence, Aspatore publishes critical tools—need-to-read as opposed to nice-to-read books—for all business professionals.

Inside the Minds

The critically acclaimed *Inside the Minds* series provides readers of all levels with proven business intelligence from C-level executives (CEO, CFO, CTO, CMO, partner) from the world's most respected companies. Each chapter is comparable to a white paper or essay and is a future-oriented look at where an industry/profession/topic is heading and the most important issues for future success. Each author has been carefully chosen through an exhaustive selection process by the *Inside the Minds* editorial board to write a chapter for this book. *Inside the Minds* was conceived in order to give readers actual insights into the leading minds of business executives worldwide. Because so few books or other publications are actually written by executives in industry, *Inside the Minds* presents an unprecedented look at various industries and professions never before available.

Managing the Human Resources Team

Leading HR Executives on Motivating Team Members, Creating an Effective Work Environment, and Achieving a Vision

Mat #40687602

BOOK & ARTICLE IDEA SUBMISSIONS

If you are a C-Level executive, senior lawyer, or venture capitalist interested in submitting a book or article idea to the Aspatore editorial board for review, please email AspatoreAuthors@thomson.com. Aspatore is especially looking for highly specific ideas that would have a direct financial impact on behalf of a reader. Completed publications can range from 2 to 2,000 pages. Include your book/article idea, biography, and any additional pertinent information.

ISBN 1-59622-583-1
Library of Congress Control Number: 2006932281

For corrections, updates, comments or any other inquiries please email AspatoreEditorial@thomson.com.

First Printing, 2006
10 9 8 7 6 5 4 3 2 1

Managing the Human Resources Team

Leading HR Executives on Motivating Team Members, Creating an Effective Work Environment, and Achieving a Vision

CONTENTS

Allan Fox   7
SERVING AS THE COMPANY'S
"HALL MONITOR"

Stephen A. Gould   13
THE HR JOURNEY
TOWARD EXCELLENCE

Michael Keane   21
MAKING HR MATTER THROUGH
STRATEGIC DELIVERY

Margaret A. Evans, Ph.D., SPHR   31
ELEVATING HR BEYOND HIRING, FIRING,
AND PLANNING THE COMPANY PICNIC

Charlene Moore Hayes   39
HR VALUES FROM A
UNIVERSITY PERSPECTIVE

Robert J. Haertel   53
MANAGING COMPENSATION
AND BENEFITS

Terri A. Lowell   **63**
ACTIONS REALLY DO SPEAK
LOUDER THAN WORDS

Steven J. Heaslip   **73**
SUCCESSFULLY EXECUTING CHANGE

Bill Ermatinger   **79**
BUILDING CREDIBILITY
TO DRIVE SUCCESS

Jill Little   **87**
DEVELOPING AND MANAGING A
WORLD-CLASS HUMAN RESOURCES TEAM

Craig R. Gill   **99**
MANAGING HR FOR RESULTS

Serving as the Company's "Hall Monitor"

Allan Fox

Chief Human Resources Officer
The Legal Aid Society

The HR Vision

My vision for managing the human resources (HR) team is to focus on servicing the client. In the past, a lot of HR functions were strictly administrative, but that has changed. Now, HR has the unique privilege of being in the position of servicing the rest of the organization about things they care a lot about. The people in HR should understand the importance of that role and the responsibility that comes with it. The management of an HR team needs to be measured differently from that of other departments. HR is not typically considered a profit center, so goals must be established based on criteria other than generating revenues. For example, when focusing on service, goals can be established around factors such as resolution time. The HR department must actively prove that it provides value to the company. The company expects HR to be fiscally responsible, show value, and quantify what it does. The value can be measured by benchmarking the success of an internship program or by structuring the benefits programs in such a way as to maximize both benefits and money.

Management Styles

I try to be approachable and have an open-door policy with all employees, especially those on the HR team. I am an advocate of open communication and the concept of "management by walking around." In fact, my nickname in my company is the "hall monitor" because my team is spread throughout the floor we're on, and I prefer face-to-face communication to other methods—therefore, I walk the halls a lot! I try to learn and teach as much as manage. Also, because of the importance of communication, I meet every morning with the managers of each HR function (benefits, payroll, HR information systems, and employment/employee relations) as a group. This meeting could be as brief as fifteen minutes—and it usually is—but it's important that we all hear what the hot issues of the day are.

I consider serving others to be the reason we're all here. I certainly hope that shows in my work ethic and management style. You have to not only talk the talk but also walk the walk. You have to lead by example. When people have problems, you have to be not only timely but also sensitive to those problems. You won't be successful if you're not approachable, reachable, and responsive to people. That's a difficult thing for some people—because, to some, it implies a certain lack of status—but I think serving others is a noble cause. When people can embrace that, it makes them successful in HR.

Common HR Challenges

One of the biggest challenges facing HR professionals is striking an effective balance between serving employees, thinking strategically, and keeping up with administrative functions. Obviously, all of the administrative tasks such as filing must be done; and if they're not done properly, they will ultimately affect your ability to effectively service employees or serve a strategic role. But some of the administrative stuff is not perceived to be as much "fun" or as "stimulating" as the interaction with employees or doing strategic things like benefits plan design or putting together an effective appraisal system. So it's important to structure job assignments in such a way as to give members of the team some exposure to service, strategy, and administrative tasks, while leveraging their strengths. The service aspect of the job should not be sacrificed in favor of the administrative part. Another challenge you hear many HR folks talk about is the idea of getting other businesspeople connected to the organization to recognize the value of HR. But I think that responsibility rests squarely on the shoulders of the senior HR person (or people) within that organization. In order to be considered a strategic partner, HR must be able to demonstrate its value. In my department, part of our daily meetings is focused on what we are doing to add value to the organization. We measure as much as we can in areas where value can be demonstrated. For example, we have a very successful intern program. We measure the value of the intern program in a variety of ways, such as the actual value of the tasks the intern is performing based on very specific feedback we solicit from the department managers and what is saved on recruitment costs in the case of an intern who ultimately fills a regular position. On a regular basis, we discuss what we are working on, how we are servicing our clients, and how we can do better in order to prove our worth to the rest of the company.

The Importance of HR

At certain times, such as during mergers and acquisitions, when people are increasingly concerned about benefits, the HR function becomes even more important to an organization. During these times, it is critical that HR makes its efforts count and makes sure it has the right priorities set to service people and respond to their needs. When an employee calls a marketing department with a problem, it's usually a problem that affects the company. But when an employee calls the HR department with a problem, it's a problem that affects the person. This presents the HR people with unique responsibilities. If the team members care about the people and understand that, at that moment in time, that employee with a problem needs to be treated like his or her problem is the only thing "on the desk," the HR department will be successful. For example, while it's great from a company standpoint to have an extremely high accuracy rate when it comes to paying employees, as far as the employee who got paid wrong is concerned, the rest of the company's payroll means nothing. He or she wants to know how and when his or her problem will be fixed.

During challenging times, taking care of employees' needs is taking care of the company's needs, because if employees' needs are not recognized, productivity will be affected. Now, I am not suggesting that caring about employees is the sole responsibility and domain of HR. Leadership at all levels of an organization should value its employees and act accordingly. However, in my experience, HR has always been the "steward of employee concern." I once worked for a very smart executive who said she considered HR to be the "conscience" of the company. And to that end, she expected HR to set the tone with regard to making sure employees' needs were considered.

The Management Team

While at Loews, I was vice president of HR and reported to the chief financial officer. There was also a manager for each functional area: benefits, HR information systems, employee relations and recruitment, and payroll. Each manager reported directly to me. I expected each one to focus on service, to be committed to constantly improving our processes, to make sure the administrative pieces were done, and to engage in open and honest communication when problems occurred. I also expected them to understand that part of the role of manager is to develop people. The management team met together on a daily basis. This allowed us to make sure everyone was in the loop and on track in terms of what was going on. At the start of each meeting, I provided details about any upcoming business, such as timelines for any company transactions or relevant conversations I had with senior managers. I did not set specific goals for each meeting, but every manager knew to be prepared to talk about key activities in their areas. If a manager needed another manager's help, the daily meeting was the time to ask for it. As our recent merger progressed, it became a time for us to take each other's pulse.

I recently joined the Legal Aid Society in New York, an extraordinary organization whose focus is on providing legal services to those who do not have the means to get services through private law firms. Although this is a complete shift with regard to the "core function" of the organization, the mission of HR remains the same: provide service to the employee population of the organization in a way that supports the organization's overall vision.

Motivating Team Members

While I do not believe in over-glorifying expectations or giving people awards for average and expected performance, I do go out of my way to formally recognize successful team members. I take every chance to recognize accomplishment by taking people to lunch, sending out e-mails, and singling out success stories during departmental meetings. For example, a team member deserved special mention when she managed an intern program, which I mentioned earlier, and tripled the value of the program by bringing in quality interns. I made sure to point out how she brought increased value to the company's senior management. I also pushed to make sure virtually everyone on my team was eligible to participate in the management bonus programs. However, I don't believe money by itself is a great motivator compared to other types of acknowledgment. People like to be recognized for their achievements and appreciated for them by peers and managers, not just given a check, although the check certainly doesn't hurt . . . as long as it's accompanied by other forms of recognition.

The Golden Rules

The first golden rule for creating a successful team is to hire the right people. People are the company's best asset. I make sure to hire people who want to grow—people who want my job. Managers need to be secure enough to hire motivated, strong people who may be able to replace them some day, and then give them the tools they need to grow. The second golden rule is to create a clear vision. The vision should then be communicated clearly and regularly to team members. The third rule is to reward team members for their successes.

Allan Fox started his professional career with Fortunoff, a New York-based retailer. After learning the business from the ground up, working as a buyer and in store operations, he joined the human resources team. As employee relations manager, he created sales incentive programs and other pay-for-performance plans. He then moved into a generalist role, overseeing staffing, employee relations, and performance management.

After Fortunoff, Mr. Fox gained experience as a financial advisor and then as an account executive at Bernard Hodes Advertising, which was the largest recruitment advertising firm in the world at the time.

He then rejoined the world of corporate human resources when he accepted a post at Barnes & Noble, the national bookseller. Focusing on corporate staffing and customer service training for the corporate staff, Mr. Fox designed and facilitated a training program that was specifically geared toward treating every employee as a customer you could provide service to. This philosophy continued to be a central theme as Mr. Fox moved to Loews Cineplex, one of the country's largest movie exhibitors. During his tenure with Loews, where he served as vice president of human resources, Mr. Fox oversaw human resources through mergers, acquisitions, bankruptcy, and several ownership changes.

Mr. Fox is now the chief human resources officer for the Legal Aid Society in New York.

The HR Journey
toward Excellence

Stephen A. Gould

Senior Vice President, Human Resources

Purolator Courier Ltd.

Leading the HR Function

The most important thing to achieve is alignment. A key part of managing is getting the team aligned around a relatively straightforward or simple strategy and focusing on a short list of priorities within that strategy. To successfully gain alignment with a team, it's essential to listen with an open mind to suggestions and concerns before setting direction. Thereafter, we use that strategy and focus on priorities to maintain our alignment and keep going. Once alignment is achieved, I am a hands-off manager. After goals are set, I assume the team members have positive intent and that they know what they are doing, and then I let them get on with doing it. Obviously, we set up regular touch-points, but I tend to let people walk their own paths and do what they think is best based on their own skills and the needs of their own teams. Simply put, my job is to set direction and help remove barriers that get in my team's way. If specific input or help is requested or if I think I can add value based on my own experiences, of course I get as involved as necessary.

It's also important to create an atmosphere of candid feedback and shared responsibility. Being direct in communicating with my staff and expecting them to be direct with me in return is a key aspect of my approach. Amongst the senior management, shared responsibility means shared leadership for the overall team. For the team at large, it's important to create an environment where job satisfaction and professional development is seen as a shared responsibility.

Managing an HR Team

Managing a human resources (HR) team is different from managing other types of teams in two specific yet contradictory ways. HR team members set high expectations for their managers and expect the company to set low expectations for the HR team members—due to the traditional outlook business (in general) has had when it comes to HR. Those in HR generally know more than the average worker about what good management entails, so they generally have high expectations that their leaders and managers are going to be role models for the types of things they are coaching and teaching other groups. The other issue that comes up when coaching HR people, and within the HR function in general, is that HR people are defensive about their value to the company. They often feel they have to justify their existence and that the company does not value them. People within HR have self-inflicted pressure in proving they are useful to the company, and this attitude is very frustrating. One way to manage this issue is to set the bar really high. We want the team to be the gold standard within the organization and to be considered the gold standard by other organizations within the HR community. In doing so, the self-inflicted pressure becomes constructive and provides focus. It also creates a sense of passion and pride in the team's work. I try to reinforce this by encouraging the team to take credit for its accomplishments, and it's important that the "limelight," if any, is always shared.

Business First

I fell into HR even though I have more of a general business than an HR background. I try to lead the team as a businessperson and help HR lead the company forward. The company needs to see me as someone who can make a contribution as a valued businessperson, no matter what my title.

If the team is aligned with what you are trying to accomplish, they will be successful. If everyone understands the vision, or at least the strategy and priorities, that is a huge step toward success. My strategy is to ask each team member to focus on no more than three areas at a time other than their own personal and professional development. Too many HR teams have lists detailing hundreds of items they are supposed to accomplish in a given year. I tell my team members to pick three to five, do them brilliantly, and then move on to the next three to five. I do not ask them to attempt all of the items at once because while they may get them all done, they won't be done well. The key to success is to be aligned and focus on key priorities and then work on personal attributes such as teamwork and behavior. If you get the message across that your desire in life is that the team is considered a gold standard, people generally like to have that kind of high expectation made of them, and it makes them feel good to know you think they are capable of reaching such heights.

The Necessary Skills

There are several important personality characteristics that make a successful HR team member. I think having a balanced perspective is important. Strong intellect, an open mind, a strong set of values, and a sense of humor are things I really look for in HR professionals. An HR team member needs a balanced and open mind because there are always multiple sides to every story. A sense of humor is important because human nature can drive a person crazy, so having a sense of humor allows the HR person to keep perspective and not take every situation too seriously. People who have strong critical thinking, problem solving, and influencing skills are also high on my list of good team members. Part of the credibility of HR is based on solving problems other managers can't or don't want to take the time to solve. Thus, critical thinking skills are important because HR-related problems tend to be complex. Rarely will one solution solve every particular problem because every situation is different. More importantly, every individual is different and needs to be communicated to in a way he or she understands and can relate to. Having the ability to evaluate what is important in a given situation and use that information to make decisions or help a manager to make a decision is a necessity.

Roadblocks

HR's biggest challenge is itself. Business has become more demanding, and staff functions such as HR, finance, and marketing are now expected more and more to demonstrate that they add value. Due to the constant pressure to prove their value, the HR community has become overly critical of its own work. While I tell my team not to worry about proving their worth, every magazine they read contradicts me. Another challenge HR faces specific to my company is that we are in a low-margin industry. We don't have millions of dollars for solutions, so we need to be creative and practical with the funds we do possess. A different type of challenge is the tight labor market in the United States and Canada. It is difficult and time-consuming to find high-quality people. To combat this challenge, we work hard to attract and retain the best people by building an employer brand, creating better advertising for our recruiting efforts, looking at new talent outside of the traditional talent pools, and leveraging our position in the marketplace. More traditionally, we have changed compensation and benefits packages, launched a stock ownership plan for employees, and used internal employee engagement surveys to gather feedback.

The Management Team

My senior management team consists of smart people who have personal accountability for their roles but are also able to work together as a team. The team consists of a director of training and development, a director of health and safety, and a director of labor relations and HR processes who oversees labor, compensation, benefits, pension, and HR systems. I also have a director of divisional HR who leads the team of generalists across the country as well as a director of corporate communications who oversees a very specific group that handles communications, public relations, and media relations. Each team member has been involved in succession planning and is intimately familiar with the duties and functions of each director's position. I require that they all work and collaborate together, so I have tried to foster that cooperation by making sure they have each walked a mile in each other's shoes. We operate on a shared leadership model. As a team, we formally meet once a month and informally meet on a regular basis. The agenda focuses on budget, our operating plan goals, and the professional development of our team members.

Working with the CEO

I have an excellent working relationship with my CEO. We meet formally on a monthly basis, but he drops by often to discuss succession planning and talent management. He also keeps abreast of any organizational alignment issues as well as contract negotiations for labor relations. We are the largest employer of Teamsters in Canada, so the union aspects of our business are huge. As he is one of our key communicators both internally and externally, and I am in charge of communications and public relations, a frequent topic of discussion is how we are communicating our message. We have a very casual relationship that highlights the drop-in culture this company cultivates. While we have regularly scheduled individual and team meetings, everyone freely walks into each other's offices for impromptu meetings.

Motivating the Team

Motivation is not usually an issue among my team members. I am very easy-going, and I like to have fun. My work is not defined by life-or-death situations. I believe I have made good progress showing team members perspective and helping them understand that HR is a long-term game, so if they are going to work a full day, they might as well have fun doing it. However, along with the enjoyable atmosphere, there also must be open and honest communication of ideas and issues.

Helpful Advice

The best piece of advice I frequently share with my team members is that the world will keep spinning tomorrow regardless of what happens today at work. I try to get them to look at the big picture and keep their perspective on what is important versus what is unimportant. I try to make sure they understand that this philosophy should be embraced from a business as well as a personal standpoint. People tend to become so involved with trivial problems at work that they forget that friends, family, and outside activities are equally as important.

Rewards Programs

We do not have a formalized recognition or rewards program for direct reports. Informally, I will take high-performing team members and their spouses out to dinner or share tickets to sporting events that the company acquires. Monetary rewards are reserved for very influential and specific achievements. For example, after negotiating our biggest collective agreement to a successful conclusion, I gave the chief negotiator a significant bonus as a surprise for a job well done. Similar types of spontaneous awards have been made for other special projects such as merger and acquisition activity. Most often, I stick to informal rewards given on a fairly regular basis.

Golden Rules

There are three golden rules for creating and managing a successful HR team. The first rule is to hold the team to a high standard that will inspire them to be the best. As a side note to that rule, the senior management team members should act as role models for the organization and show how aiming for the gold standard will lead to success. The second rule is to keep perspective and keep an eye on the big picture and the long term. The third golden rule is to take the high road, stick to your core values, and never settle. Always assume positive intent and give the benefit of the doubt.

As senior vice president of human resources for Purolator, Stephen A. Gould has responsibility for all aspects of human resources including business strategy, organizational design, talent management and succession planning, performance management, compensation and benefits, pension, management development, operations training, and employee and labor relations. He is also responsible for environment, health, and safety and corporate communications, which includes employee communications, public affairs, and corporate philanthropy.

Mr. Gould serves as the management lead on the Purolator board of directors' compensation and human resources committee, pension committee, and environment, health, and safety committee. He is also Purolator's privacy compliance officer.

Prior to joining Purolator, Mr. Gould was vice president of human resources for Amex Canada Inc. He also held other positions at PepsiCo, McDonnell Douglas Canada, and Ernst & Young.

Mr. Gould holds a B.A., with honors, in economics from the University of Toronto and an M.S. in industrial relations from the London School of Economics at the University of London. He is a member of the boards of directors of the Toronto Children's Breakfast Club and the Huntington Society of Canada.

Making HR Matter through Strategic Delivery

Michael Keane
Senior Vice President, Human Resources Strategy Delivery
Limited Brands Inc.

Putting the HR Team Together

More than anything else, I look for courage in prospective team members. I want people who know what they believe, are true to their belief systems, and have the ability to articulate their visions, even when someone with a big title challenges them. The rationale is simple—you can't be a good human resources (HR) person if the only things you believe in are driven by senior leaders' beliefs. This doesn't mean you have to be obnoxious or obstinate; it means you have to stand up for yourself and, many times, others.

The second dimension I look for in team members is a pattern of being able to connect their work to the business while creating meaningful relationships with leaders. I ask people to tell me about their two best clients and describe the issues about which those clients call them. If someone tells me his or her clients only call regarding HR practices (e.g., performance reviews, disciplinary issues, staffing advice), I know he or she is probably a decent HR team member. If, however, this person is getting calls about all kinds of business matters, that tells me he or she is probably a great HR team member. If HR people get invited to meetings that don't have an obvious organizational issue attached to them, it means they're regarded as good thought partners. Those are the people I'm looking for.

Last, I look for "difference makers," whom I define as people who do their job but are not bound by their job description. These are people who are thinking all the time about what really matters to the business and associates, and how they can influence those outcomes. Combined with courage and relevance to the business, you have a powerful HR person in the making.

Once we have put the people on the team who exhibit the attributes of courage, business relevance, and a pattern of making a difference, we focus new HR team members on creating a reputation for being highly responsive. If your clients don't think you can deliver on small things, you're never going to get their attention on big things. You need to establish a baseline of credibility through responsiveness. As our vice chairman has said, "People don't care what you know until they know you care." Responding consistently and quickly creates the valid impression that you care, which opens the door for the HR advisor.

While responsiveness makes it possible for HR people to get heard by their clients, it takes "another level" of skill to truly connect with leaders. This is the number-one career derailer for otherwise talented HR professionals. The most effective HR people understand they are not fighting for budget or prestige. Rather, they are fighting for share of their clients' minds and energy—it's all about whether you can influence leaders and hold their attention.

Management Style and Substance: Setting Direction and Establishing Trust

Identifying Priorities

It's the leader's job to generate the starting list of HR priorities. A huge part of that lies in translating the business growth strategies and leadership's articulated needs into organizational outcomes. I am ultimately accountable for identifying our customers and determining what they expect from us. My job is also about implementing management systems, which is an ongoing process by which we determine exactly what we're measuring.

At the end of the day, our job in HR is no different from a marketer in a consumer packaged goods company or a merchant in a retailer. Give the customers what they need and want. The starting point is, obviously, "What do they want?" Customers—internal and external—speak in code. They don't tell us exactly what they need. Sometimes they are clear, but by and large, my job is to lead the HR team in deciphering their wishes, balancing them against the organization's stated financial and strategic goals, and defining how we can contribute to their success.

At Limited Brands Inc., as in many organizations, we want our people focused on the work that will most affect the customer's response to our brands in a financial manner. To help achieve that, we use a concept called "Critical Few Initiatives." We pursue only a few strategies at once. These strategies reflect our unique role in the organization as well as what the organization needs during a certain period of its life. We have a set of initiatives to support the brand growth plan. I've also lived in organizations that used the concepts of the "Balanced Scorecard," but the principles are the same.

Part of HR's unique role is to help manage change, so our annual goals always reflect support of several of the most significant change initiatives impacting the organization. For example, we are one of the lead functions in an initiative to change how the Express denim business is executed. We're creating a brand new product development model for denim, which is a high-growth business for the brand. By co-locating resources in design, merchandising, and manufacturing, we believe we can become faster to market and more responsive to changing consumer trends. If so, this would lead to lower markdowns, because we're closer to the fashion curve—lots of dollars attached to that outcome.

Our HR initiative is to support the population of the denim design team with new talent and help shepherd the larger change process, covering everything from the redefinition of the product development milestone calendar, to the process redesign, to the creation of new office space. At its most simple level, some would say, "You're just moving four jobs from New York to Columbus. What's the big deal?" When you think about what it will take to make this change successful, however, it's more complex and demanding. Effective HR teams get this and support the change appropriately.

As it regards the multiyear HR strategy, we are clearly focused on three areas: leader development, talent pool management, and change support.

We have a standing set of initiatives to create a great leadership group. Our organization is significantly driven by the quality of our leadership. We have to determine whether we have enough leadership capacity and to assess the behaviors our leaders exhibit. We need to know what kind of culture our leaders create, because no matter what you say your culture and values are, "The culture is what the leaders do." Consequently, we need to know what our leaders do, how those behaviors support the intended environment, and what steps we should be taking, broadly or narrowly, to get more alignment. We have an entire set of leadership effectiveness and culture-building initiatives with training and development components.

Like any HR function, we have a leadership role in acquiring talent that is connected to our strategies. We're also responsible for defining and implementing development mechanisms to bridge the gaps between what we have and what we need. Taken together, this is probably the most associate-centric work we do each year.

As I mentioned in the denim design example, we always have initiatives to support major organization change work. In addition, we have an internal communications agenda to help build the culture, reinforce key leadership messages, and prepare the organization for the next wave of change.

Our initiative specifics vary from year to year, but everything revolves around where we are and where we want to go. Goal setting doesn't have to be over-intellectualized and unnecessarily challenging. The important thing is to set targets that are meaningful and time-bound.

Establishing Trust with the Team

It's obvious to say trust is important—to argue the opposite would be shortsighted. The challenge for any leader is how you build that with your team. In my experience of leading and coaching leaders, there are three important truths about building trust and, ultimately, loyalty:

1. You have to be credible in your content—people will follow you in the belief that doing so will get them to a better place. My team is willing to follow my lead because they believe I am engaged in what the business is doing. They see and sense the credibility I have with other business leaders. This makes it easier to accept that our work will be valued.
2. You clearly serve your team as the path to getting them to serve you, primarily by setting clear direction and continually helping clear obstacles to their success.
3. You show you care about your team, as people.

Leaders often seek "loyalty" in their teams, and I find the best leaders understand that you get loyalty when you exhibit it yourself. I am highly committed to generating loyalty in this manner. When I got my job leading the HR team at Express, it was in a summary (i.e., happened in a single morning) fashion. I was very different from the person who held the position before me, so I had to earn loyalty. I spent time talking about the spirit in which we work. I talked about what it means to be honest, direct, and respectful of the people we serve. I made one simple request and commitment to my people. Once we had spent reasonable time defining the spirit in which we would work, all I asked of them is that they respect that spirit. If they did so, and work they were doing did not turn out well, my commitment to them was that I would take at least the first bullet, if not all of them. If, however, they stepped outside of our agreement, we would have a much different conversation. I had great success with this approach. I have taken bullets and expect I will again in the future.

Managing the Team for Results

With goals and strategies established, my primary role throughout the year is to ensure that we stay on track to achieve those goals. I look at what our measurements are telling us and consider the implications. I assess our learning environment in HR. One of the most important things I do is determine when we're doing something we shouldn't be doing. My management style is metrics-oriented, with the business first and the HR team second.

Our HR teams are obviously focused on helping all leaders achieve their goals, no matter what part of the organization they're in. In retail, we live in a metrics-driven world where we know exactly how we did each day, sometimes in two-hour increments. Every week, we essentially re-plan our business. Being relevant in this environment requires an HR team to be metrics-centric, because everyone else is. This can be uncomfortable for some HR people, but it's part of the change process through which we are embarking.

Using Metrics to Tell a Story

We have our own HR scorecard, which we track each month of the year. We report the results to the organization and break everything down by functional group. Our goal is to increase accountability for our functional leaders. We call this "organization health" analysis.

All of our metrics are captured at the total brand level, and then we break the numbers down for each functional area. Everyone gets the information at the same time. We then rely on the inherent competitiveness of people. Once people start to feel like they're being supported rather than simply measured, they can get with the program pretty quickly.

The key issue with the scorecard and metrics is not in the spreadsheet's elegant construction or whether there are a few "more perfect" measures. The numbers are numbers, in and of themselves. The challenge for the HR team is in making the numbers tell a story. People love to hear stories, even as adults. Leaders especially love to hear stories about the organization to which they devote so much energy trying to lead. When new people start working with us on the scorecard, getting them to the numbers is usually not the issue. The challenge is in helping them tease out the story the numbers weave together—the story is in there, but it has to be found and articulated.

Making Progress and Learning Concurrently

In our business unit HR structure, our key players are the directors of HR for the stores and home office, for each brand. Each of those directors has some combination of managers, generalists, and/or coordinators reporting to him or her. Many HR teams also have a director of internal communications.

The HR teams have formal meetings every week. I have a touching base meeting with my direct reports every Monday or Tuesday that is focused on the big issues carrying over from the week before as well as new issues for the upcoming week. My direct reports, in turn, meet with their teams on Monday or Tuesday. These meetings are meant to maintain focus on the major HR initiatives and/or significant brand business challenges. They keep up with the daily flow of work and make progress against initiatives in this manner—we know what's due when, and we touch base to check up on deadlines.

The management of the weekly issues is clearly urgent, but doing only this creates the possibility that you end up inadvertently minimizing time on the important work. This is certainly relevant to my role involving multiple brands, where I can't be in any brand all the time.

To deal with this issue, I happened upon a wonderful process we call the "deep dive" meeting. By dividing my teams into their natural intact work groups, I meet with them each month on a topic of their choosing. The agenda and topic is theirs. If there is something I should be preparing for or reading in advance, they let me know. We meet for two and a half hours, which is an exceedingly long time in our environment. This has turned into one of the most powerful unintended learning experiences of my career.

I originally conceived the deep dive meetings in part for group learning but also for my own selfish purposes, so I could get brought fully up to speed on my teams' work, at a lower level of detail, in the event I was questioned by senior leaders. I loosely sketched out the nature of the topics we should discuss—critical HR initiatives, talent agenda, emerging brand strategic issues, etc.—and then let the teams drive each meeting.

What a great deal it has turned out to be. What started as a "What does the boss want?" exercise quickly evolved into a free-flowing venue for all of us in HR to gather and discuss the most important issues we face. One month it was how to help drive business process improvement, the next month the major change communication messages for the upcoming meeting with all store managers, and the next month a wide-ranging discussion about a brand learning and development platform.

In short, what started out as an attempt to get the leader the information he wanted turned into a group learning event that makes each related initiative better conceived and better executed. In addition, we all learn more about what we do without having to attend an external course or figure out how to apply to our work—all our learning is contextualized in our own organization, and the people we are serving.

The deep dive process, as it were, works for two simple reasons. First, its content is driven by the people closest to the work, which means we are rarely spending time on stuff that just doesn't matter. Second, it offers an overt opportunity to push the "pause" button, take a breath, and evaluate how and why we do certain things the way we do. Businesses don't generally allow you to do that, so it's important that you engineer mechanisms for doing so with the team.

Getting People to Work Together

You can have a great HR strategy, linked to the business strategy. You can have wonderful metrics and talent initiatives that make sense for the brand. Whatever target the HR team is shooting at, it does not matter if the group does not consistently execute. There is an old saying: "Retail is detail." The statement may not rhyme as sweetly, but it is just as applicable to any industry. HR teams that execute consistently are often the most collaborative ones.

As an HR leader—or business leader, for that matter—who is focused on getting consistent execution, I'm maniacally focused on creating an environment of individual accountability balanced with collaborative support. Teams that can't collaborate stumble. If I'm a generalist serving the marketing and sales clients, I should want the generalist who supports the manufacturing team to be just as successful as I am. Why? Because his or her success makes it easier for me to sell my clients on how my proposals will lead to their success. My teammates' success only helps the "brand" of the HR function, which helps me. If I don't see things that way, there's a big problem brewing, and it's just a matter of time until it breaks the surface.

At the end of the day, the customers don't differentiate whether HR is good or bad. If an HR team thinks it can win by making its colleagues less successful, that team is sorely mistaken.

Michael Keane is senior vice president of human resources strategy delivery for Limited Brands Inc., the world's foremost specialty retailer. In this role, he is accountable for the conceptualization and delivery of human resources services in each of the corporation's eight brands, including Victoria's Secret, Bath & Body Works, Express, Limited Stores, White Barn Candle Company, and Henri Bendel, among others. These brands collectively employ almost 100,000 associates and operate more than 3,400 stores, two Internet businesses, and one catalog business.

Mr. Keane joined Limited Brands Inc. in 2000 as director of human resources for the Structure brand and was promoted to vice president of human resources of the Express business in 2001 with oversight for both home office and stores. In 2005, he was promoted to group vice president of human resources for the Apparel Group. He assumed his current duties in 2006.

Prior to joining Limited Brands Inc., Mr. Keane was director of associate development at Borden Foods Corporation for five years, and prior to that, he held various human resource and marketing positions over five years for the Whirlpool Corporation.

Mr. Keane received his B.A. in American studies from the University of Notre Dame and his M.B.A. from Indiana University.

Dedication: *I dedicate this chapter to my parents, William and Mary Joy Keane, who taught me the value of service to others that underpins all my work, and to my wife, Katy, who convinced me I had something to say.*

Elevating HR Beyond Hiring, Firing, and Planning the Company Picnic

Margaret A. Evans, Ph.D., SPHR

Director, Human Resources

Government Employees Hospital Association Inc.

As the director of human resources (HR) for a national health insurance provider, I am charged with the responsibility of managing my company's most valuable asset—its employees. With the ever-changing landscape of the employer/employee relationship, this task has become more of an integral part of my company's fiscal success than ever before, making it essential to motivate my department and other company executives to look beyond the obvious administrative role of a traditional HR department and focus more on the strategic and economic value my department adds by working to successfully retain, develop, engage, and inspire employees.

While there is little new about this approach to HR management in theory, it continues to be a completely new concept in day-to-day practice and application. Most HR departments around the nation are tucked away—only interacting to employ, terminate, train, or mediate. Yet, the HR department should be more than a task shop that hires and fires, administers benefits, and plans the corporate picnic. My vision for my department, and HR departments overall, is to have a more strategic voice in the boardroom as the critical link between the company's workforce and its profitability. Achieving this vision requires a new way of thinking about the function of HR, a more deliberate approach that steps back from day-to-day tasks and asks the question: "How does this help our employees contribute to the bottom line?"

Achieving the Vision

The first step toward achieving this vision in my department involved doing something typical of HR departments—developing a mission statement. However, my department's atypical next step is what has led to our success. Instead of filing the mission statement away to collect dust, we have been successful because we continue to have regular strategic and corporate planning meetings to help remind us of the importance of our mission and its impact on our employees, our customers, and ultimately our viability as a company. While most companies take this type of reflective look just once a year, we convene monthly to get a clear vision of our purpose and align our performance with that vision.

What types of tangible changes have resulted from this monthly checkup? One major change was my department's involvement in the company's technological upgrades. Historically, decisions about technology at my company, and at many companies, only involve finance and the information technology department. This approach often overlooks the human component of the decision-making process by focusing solely on the technology's function and cost. In keeping with our mission, my department was able to add value by making a case for our early involvement in the decision-making process to help keep several unconsidered factors in the forefront. These were factors that typically are an afterthought once the technology is already purchased and installed, such as: Do our employees have the skill set and training required to use the technology? If not, how long will it take to get them up to speed? How will this training process affect the company's ability to serve its customers? How can we keep morale and productivity high during the transition? These questions are all too often asked so late in the process that effective implementation becomes an arduous task for both employees and the information technology department.

Another important realization that resulted from our monthly check-up meetings was that we lacked measurement tools that showed how our department's performance impacted the bottom line. How could we actually know if we were successful in our mission and demand a greater voice in executive decision-making if we could not show how our involvement saved money or increased employee performance? The simple answer is that we could not. Our solution spawned an insightful report that measures factors like the retention of new hires and the time required to fill positions in order to determine the cost per hire. This hard data allows us to look at processes analytically and develop ways to manage hiring more cost-effectively.

Using careful analysis to drive decisions also helped our department review the success of the company's wellness initiatives. By thinking strategically, we were able to eliminate the fat, so to speak, by cutting programs that sounded good in a benefits brochure but failed to affect employee productivity. At the heart of our wellness initiatives today is the question: "Does this program positively affect the rate of sick days, absenteeism, medical plan usage, employee satisfaction, and so on?" This type of strategic thinking and evaluating surpasses routine HR duties and allows our department to know precisely how we add value to the company.

Team Characteristics Required to Achieve the Vision

Functioning with this new approach to HR requires a team of hard workers, problem solvers, collaborators, and relationship builders. I set the bar high for my staff of ten employees (five of whom are HR specialists) and let them know I expect them to take initiative to propose and lead projects, be flexible and willing to learn new systems, and follow different strategies.

When I conducted interviews for my staff, I met with each candidate and asked them a series of questions to help me to understand their personality and goals and to determine whether they were a good fit for the department. I also used their applications and profiles to understand where they were professionally. An employee who was too set in his or her way of looking at HR based on previous experiences would not fit well. Having the right people on board has been critical to my department's success and cannot be overlooked as an important driver of strategic HR management.

My staff and I develop short- and long-term goals and set expectations annually. I allow them enough latitude to perform their assignments without micromanagement and maintain an open-door policy to identify issues before they become problematic. As a result, my staff and I have mutual trust and are willing and able to successfully rebound when a mistake is made or additional training is required to improve in areas where we may fall short. As their leader, I hold myself to the same high standards I expect from them, and I challenge myself to remain flexible enough to manage in different ways depending on the situation and the individual.

Measuring the Contribution of Individual Team Members

The old cliché is true—we are only as strong as our weakest link. As such, I have found that it is critical to break down my department's performance on an individual level. Each team member must review and submit his or her individual goals every fourth quarter. I review these goals one on one with each employee, and then we review them together as a department. The entire team decides what we believe are realistic goals for each area. This 360-degree approach fosters buy-in and results in everyone working together. We track our progress using our company's measurement terms of "maximum," "par," and "threshold" performance.

My department's two employment specialists provide a good example of this measurement process. Their effectiveness is measured by the average amount of time it takes them to fill positions from posting to hire date. The benchmark may be to fill 75 percent of the positions within six weeks to meet maximum performance, 50 percent of the positions within six weeks for par, and less than 50 percent for threshold.

Another measurable goal for our employment specialists is completion of new employee orientation follow-ups. Here, 75 percent of all new hires should attend a follow-up orientation within six months of hire to meet the maximum goal, 50 percent of all employees should attend a follow-up orientation within six weeks to meet par, and less than 50 percent attendance is considered threshold.

My department's trainers follow suit with their measurement criteria. They are evaluated based on the quality of training programs. This is measured using attendee evaluations. A 75 percent overall favorable response meets the maximum goal, a 50 percent overall favorable response meets par performance, and less than 50 percent is threshold.

To help team members who function in specialist or professional capacities achieve maximum performance, I have continuing education requirements. All professionals must become certified in some area. It is my belief that certification helps them remain professionally competent by requiring them to continuously take courses in their area of expertise and challenging them to excel. It is also my expectation that members of my staff maintain membership in at least one professional organization (paid for by the company) and actively participate in that organization by volunteering in some way.

For example, my department's compensation specialist regularly attends conferences to maintain certification as a senior professional in HR and keep abreast of trends in pay for performance to ensure that we stay in sync with salary surveys and the current labor market in our pay structure.

Because my staff members know they will be accountable for meeting performance measurements and ongoing training requirements, they stay sharp and have confidence in their professional competence, which is an excellent boost to my department's morale.

Establishing a Proactive Relationship with Senior Management

Instead of functioning as the sole liaison between HR and other department leaders, I encourage my staff to establish proactive relationships with my company's senior management team. The specialists on my team, as well as the company's line managers, should be jointly responsible for getting the workforce to execute company strategy and tactics, and thus should have positive working relationships to accomplish this goal.

To help them better interact outside of the department, my HR professionals are expected to learn the business and understand the company's financial situation by learning how to analyze budgets, read the financial statements and reports, and translate those into specific actions and accountabilities. With this expanded knowledge base, HR can be proactive with management and help forecast issues that will help the company with strategic planning. For example, understanding our company's business allowed my department to make our executive committee aware of the threat of Avian Flu to our business. We challenged them to consider the strategic impact a potential crisis would have on our prescription drugs, health claims, and communications with our customers. When HR communicates concerns of this nature to senior management, we show that we are not just thinking of our employees but about the overall picture.

Ongoing Challenges

While my department has enjoyed significant success by adhering to our mission, we continue to experience a number of challenges. First and foremost, we are still working to change the negative Big Brother perception some employees have tied to the HR department. While we do serve as the company's gatekeeper, we must continue to bridge those gaps in perception within the organization, so we can be viewed as a collaborative part of the corporate team.

Secondly, there are important HR functions that still fail to get fully integrated into the strategic planning and operational framework of the company. For example, the HR department should be consulted during budget planning to offer expertise on the financial impact of workplace laws on company benefit and retirement plans as well as the cost of adhering to heath and safety regulations mandated under the Occupational Safety and Health Administration and other federal legislation.

My department, as well as other HR departments nationwide, will have to work through the challenges of benefit designs as health care and other costs continue to rise. Our aging workforce also needs to become a greater consideration in corporate strategic planning. According to the Society of Human Resource Management, America's workforce is older than ever before, and as retirement nears for 76 million baby boomers, companies like mine will be "bracing for difficulty in staffing highly skilled and senior jobs and looking for ways to retain older workers."

Dr. Margaret A. Evans is the director of human resources for Government Employees Hospital Association Inc., a national health insurance plan that provides comprehensive medical benefits to more than 420,000 federal employees and their dependent family members. Since 1987, she has successfully worked to foster a positive work environment that supports employee development and helps achieve the company's fiscal goals and objectives.

In addition to her service as a human resources executive, Dr. Evans has made significant contributions to the human resources field through her active involvement in professional human resources organizations both nationally and locally. At the national level, she served as a national board member for the Society of Human Resource Management for five consecutive years and was the group's regional vice president for Area IV prior to serving on the board. From 1989 to 1998, she was appointed to the organization's national research committee and was instrumental in bringing to the forefront the finest empirical research in the field through her participation in the planning and directing of the annual Creative Application and Research Awards and the annual Book Award Program.

Locally, Dr. Evans has actively participated since 1977 on several committees for the Human Resource Management Association of Greater Kansas City. Along with her election as chapter president in 1998, Dr. Evans has also served locally as the secretary/treasurer of both the Missouri State Council and the Human Resource Certification Board. She also helped set professional testing criteria for certified human resources professionals as the exam development director for the Human Resource Certification Board between 1994 and 1995.

Outside of her career contributions, Dr. Evans devotes considerable time and resources to several civic and philanthropic organizations. She is a member of the board of directors of the Greater Pentecostal Temple, a life member of the National Association for the Advancement of Colored People, a life member of the Jackson County, Missouri, chapter of the Links Inc., and a member of Alpha Kappa Alpha Sorority Inc., where she has been elected president, vice president, secretary, recording secretary, and parliamentarian. Currently, she serves on the Alpha Kappa Alpha national human resource committee.

Dr. Evans holds a doctoral degree in business administration as well as a graduate degree in public administration and an undergraduate degree in psychology from the University of Missouri at Kansas City. She resides in Kansas City, where she enjoys spending time with her two sons and four grandchildren.

Acknowledgment: *My sincerest thanks go to my niece, Monica L. White, who continues to be a valuable editorial voice throughout all of my publishing endeavors. I am also indebted to my colleague, LouAnne Jensen, for her assistance in providing helpful research that supports my writing. Finally, to my children, Carl and Chris: your love and support allow me to continue striving for excellence.*

HR Values from a University Perspective

Charlene Moore Hayes

Vice President, Human Resources

The Johns Hopkins University

A Look at Our Team

We have a highly collaborative human resources (HR) team. I always try to reach a consensus on decisions with my team members. We raise questions, identify issues, and reach better solutions when we have the entire management team involved in the decision-making process.

I'm not afraid to make a decision on my own. If it's abundantly clear that we can't reach a consensus as a team, I will use the information I gathered from the team to make a call. Either way, I am confident I end up with a better decision than I would have reached alone.

I am not a micromanager. It's important to give people the room to manage their own functions, lead their own groups, and do their jobs the best way they can. It's also important to be supportive. I let people do their jobs and touch base regularly. One of my team members recently commented that as a leader, I offer just the right amount of support, encouragement, and advice, while providing the needed strategic direction.

I meet with each member of my management team at least biweekly to keep myself informed and make sure we're all on the same track. I believe it's important to support my leadership team. I try to ensure that people have the resources they need to do their jobs, and I encourage their own development.

I believe in values-based leadership and leading by example. Excellence in practice and service, respect, honesty, integrity, diversity of thought and people, creativity, and innovation are all values I hold dearly and communicate as important to my team. I work hard to demonstrate these values as a matter of course. I don't expect perfection, but I do expect that each of us will constantly strive for it. While I don't celebrate mistakes, I do believe mistakes can serve the organization well as long as the lessons learned are shared with others in the organization and we are proactive in our efforts to avoid repeating them in the future. I don't hesitate to admit my own mistakes, and I focus equal attention on ensuring that I learn from those lessons.

Relationship building is also an important part of my leadership style. While it comes naturally to me, I make it a point to build strong relationships throughout the organization. With nearly 200 people on my decentralized HR team and new people coming into the organization constantly, meeting each of them is important to me. I take thirty minutes to an hour to get to know a little something about them personally. It helps me understand what is important to them, what motivates them, and what development or opportunities might be right for them in the future.

I extend my relationships beyond the HR team to others at all levels of the university. I meet them in their spaces, pay attention to topics or issues that are important to them, and engage on a personal level in ways that are surprising to them. Employees in support positions within the organization are surprised when I accept an invitation to join them and their families for a holiday meal or to attend a special event in which they are featured. Faculty members are surprised to see me in the audience at one of their lectures or attending a symposium. I sometimes shock the dean of our music conservatory by showing up at a student recital or composition reading. Yet, as a fully participating citizen of the university and executive-level officer, I see it as my basic responsibility to be involved and understand generally the work of our employees, including the faculty. This approach to leadership has been extremely helpful to me. There are people throughout the organization to whom I can turn for information, advice, or assistance. Because of the relationships I build, I am rarely met with resistance. It's important to understand what is going on in every area of the university in order to make a contribution to the mission of the organization.

My Team and Its Vision

My immediate team consists of subject matter experts in the organization and top-level generalists. It's my hope that people will turn to my team members for solutions and view them as experts in their particular areas. Those areas include compensation, benefits, employee and organization development, leadership development or talent management, employee and labor relations, and general day-to-day people management. My vision is that each of them is assumed to be a significant strategic partner with leaders of the organizational segment he or she serves. I also envision a team that can move from a strategic partnership to organizational leadership, helping to define and create a high-performance organization.

The centralized subject matter experts must be constantly aware of industry and workforce trends, best practices, organizational goals, and values. They must be predictors of the future, strategists, and/or planners who help ensure that we have the policies, processes, and systems in place to attract, retain, and develop the workforce we need for the future. These subject matter experts help us stay ahead of the curve.

A lot of organizations have an organizational development staff. We are no different, but my vision is that more and more of our HR leaders are also organizational development experts to the extent that they exhibit the knowledge and skills necessary to facilitate the creation of a high-performance organization. We cannot afford to limit those skills to a talented few. Our organization is too large and too complex.

The HR generalists who are distributed throughout the university must constantly have their fingers on the pulse of their segments of the organization. They must be resourceful, calling on the central subject matter experts and other generalists for support and advice. They must understand the business of the unit and know well the laws, rules, regulations, and polices impacting HR management. Our generalists are the HR leaders who facilitate problem solving daily and focus constantly on enabling managers to do their jobs and on creating a work environment that inspires employees to contribute at the highest levels possible.

It is easy to put HR executives into two different buckets. Higher education is very different from the corporate world. HR executives in corporations have long understood the need to know the business in order to impact the bottom line. The corporate profit motive helps drive that home. In higher education, we now realize that as non-profits, it is also important to know the business in order to determine where we can add value.

The culture of higher education is traditional. Even today, it is difficult to use business taxonomy in discussions about how we ensure quality education for our students or provide top-notch service to our internal and external customers. It is even more difficult for us to talk about managing a bottom line, so HR executives in higher education often see their roles solely as managing processes, contributing to the benefit strategy, and creating a pool of applicants for open positions. We have got to move beyond the tactical to understand what it means in our world to manage the bottom line.

Defining Success

I've been here for two and a half years. In this environment, people don't like to talk about customer satisfaction, but the first thing I tackled when I came on board was process improvement. If everyone is complaining about what we do, then we're not serving anyone well.

When I came into the organization, I heard from everybody who had touched our employment process that there were problems. The process wasn't working for anyone, yet we were putting a lot of money into it. We eventually got to a point where there was a significant reduction of complaints from applicants, recruiters felt like they had the tools they needed to do a better job, and managers felt like they had a system that would help them find the best person for the job. That, to me, defines success.

We are responsive to the needs of each of our constituent groups. We strive to improve constantly their experience. That is one indicator of success. Another indicator falls more along quantitative business lines. One of the challenges we face is the rising cost of medical care and other benefits. Higher education is not the best-paying employer group, but we pride ourselves on our benefits. When you add salaries to benefits packages and look at total compensation, we stack up well.

The key to our success in this area is to manage effectively the cost of our benefits, while retaining the high value of our benefits program. One of the challenges we have is that the cost of medical care is rising rapidly. The prescription drug price is growing faster than any other factor. If we can continue to provide a benefits package that helps us maintain an edge when it comes to our peers in a way that allows the university to save money or constrain costs, we will consider ourselves successful.

Strategies for Success

I attribute my success to a number of factors. First, I focus always on improving the HR experience for each leader, manager, and employee who touches our services. I always hit the ground looking for the lowest-hanging fruit. In my current position, I found that fruit in our recruitment area. Our employment system caused the greatest angst for all of our constituents. Improving that system became one of my top priorities. We had an excellent replacement up and running within the first ten months of my appointment and saved the university a significant sum of money.

Using that same principle, I identified my remaining priorities, including a new pay system, a university-wide performance management system to serve as a foundation for talent management, and other process improvements throughout the organization. Beyond these improvements, the university's leaders identified the need to better manage our benefits cost as a major expectation for me.

Second, I focus on issues beyond the HR operation. The faculty is used to seeing me at lectures and other events outside my realm of responsibility.

One of the criticisms from the academic side of the house is that HR doesn't typically understand the needs of faculty. I relate that to understanding the business because we are in the business of teaching, research, and patient care—all part of our academic missions.

My focus has helped me to be successful because people see me as someone who understands their challenges. They see me participating in venues that are important to them. They are more apt to trust me as a sounding board and view me as someone who can help them solve their problems. More importantly, they trust me to help define the direction of the organization.

Third, I communicate transparently, seek input widely, and encourage the participation of all those who are ultimately affected by our organizational decisions. That is the surest way to gain credibility and buy-in for my strategic direction and tactical approaches. Even those who don't agree with the outcomes appreciate and understand the reasons for the decisions.

Fourth and finally, I believe in surrounding myself with top-notch people, often with skills that far exceed my own and strengths to which I aspire. I look for team members who complement my skills and share my values. I don't compromise on talent. Once I identify a staffing need, I base the competencies I seek on the organization's needs, and seek to find the very best talent available to join me. My team members are a huge part of my success.

Working as a Team

Not all of my team members need to have the broad view that I do, but I want the directors of our divisional offices to understand their divisions the same way I seek to understand the overall university. The same applies to the people who are in our centers of expertise like compensation, benefits, organizational development, labor, and employee relations. I want them to be aware of the overall needs of the university and to know how their piece fits into the organization. They must also have an understanding of the relationship between and among their units and other areas of HR. We cannot operate in silos or in a vacuum.

My leadership team meets every two weeks. Because we are implementing an enterprise resource planning system, there are stretches of time when more frequent meetings are necessary. During the critical stages of the project, it is important that we are ready and able to make quick decisions and that we are in a position to support each other and the project team.

We all need to understand the overall challenges and goals of the university, and we need to work together to make sure we're integrated. My expectation is that we work together as a team and integrate our services so that when people view an HR leader, they see a person who represents the values of the entire organization.

Key Players

I have a senior director of human services whose role includes leadership development, organizational development and diversity, career management, training and development, employee assistance, and work/life balance. I think of human services as the area that takes care of the organization's health and the personal and professional development of our employees. In many ways, employees in the office of human services help shape our organization's future. Currently, this senior director is helping me think through talent management strategies. I often take advantage of his executive coaching skills.

The office of human services is our biggest central group because organizational and professional development is so important to the organization. Our training group is very strong as well. We spend a lot of time and money on training and career management. I have a senior director for labor and employee relations. This person administers our labor contracts. She negotiates the agreement in conjunction with legal counsel, manages our grievance process, and is responsible for policy development.

My senior director of benefits planning and administration is focused on our benefits program and ensures that we have a competitive and cost-effective package to attract and retain employees. With the help of an advisory committee, we developed a benefits philosophy to help guide our decisions as we make improvements to our benefits program. Among other things, we are looking at opportunities to realize savings on prescription drugs as a major piece of our overall cost-reduction strategy. The director is also focusing a lot of attention on wellness programs in an effort to get our employees to take better care of themselves. We realize that educating our employees and increasing wellness and preventive care have the greatest potential for cutting overall medical care costs.

The benefits director and compensation director are both working to help employees understand their total compensation or total rewards, as we have begun to call it. We produce and issue annual total rewards statements that illustrate in dollars and cents the total value of the salary and benefits provided by the university to each employee.

My compensation director is spending most of her time now on implementing a new pay program. We are moving away from a decades-old knowledge and abilities classification system to a more nimble system that focuses on the employee's role in and contribution to the organization. This new pay system will have a tighter connection to the market, helping us keep pace with the market and enabling managers to reward employees for performance, increased skills, and competencies without looking for ways to redefine their positions.

We will no longer have members of our compensation staff spending valuable time on detailed job descriptions, trying to make minute distinctions between positions and grade levels. Instead, our compensation group will add more value to the organization by ensuring that we understand the market and are in a position to respond quickly. They will be available to provide special studies for managers and continually work to ensure that our pay practices are effectively meeting our organization's needs. This new system will help reinforce our organizational values and lay the groundwork for a more deliberate, comprehensive plan for talent management. It is a totally new way of valuing the work of our employees—a significant culture shift that requires a great deal of attention to change management. Because of its significance, we are relying heavily on input and advice from leaders across the university. Facilitating the culture shift required for this new pay program is certain to be an even bigger challenge than the program design.

As a team, we do not shy away from multiple projects. The senior director for benefits is also taking the lead on establishing an HR transaction center. This center will be a shared services center managed by the university and servicing the university, hospital, and health system. The center will open with the implementation of our enterprise resource planning system in early 2007 and is a direct result of the planning associated with that information systems project. All benefits and personnel actions will flow through the transaction center. This new center will begin the process of shifting the transactional work historically handled by HR professionals to a central location, eventually freeing up the HR managers and generalists to do more value-added work and creating more effective and efficient processes.

I have divisional HR directors who are generalists. These generalists assist particular divisions of the university with all of their HR needs. They help employees and managers access central resources and oversee tactical work while remaining part of the strategic team. There is someone who focuses on compensation and classification, someone who handles employee relations issues, and people who recruit employees. Each division has a divisional office led by a generalist who reports to me.

In our larger schools, we have matrixed reporting. The division heads are closely tied to their deans. The heads report to the dean, who functionally reports to me. This helps ensure that the heads are on top of the things that are going on within their division. They know the business, but they are also part of the overall HR organization.

I recently created the position of financial manager. We had a huge organization with no finance person. Someone was doing the books, but there is a lot of money that goes through HR, and there was no one to focus on our finances.

With the creation of the financial manager position, we are finally beginning to quantify what we are doing. We have someone who can build a financial model and show how we're saving money administratively. We're able to show that we're saving the organization money while providing a higher level of service. The finance manager just started in January, and he has been a marvelous addition to our team.

The compensation director also leads the HR information systems group. This group takes care of our technology and produces special reports. Currently, we have a patchwork of systems that is difficult to navigate, but they pull information together. After we implement our new information system, reports should be easier for all of us to access, but the HR information systems group will continue to play a key role in helping us define the parameters of special reports. The HR information systems group includes programmers, our Web master, and others who make sure our technology is working. They do a lot of the data management and act as our internal helpdesk. It is this group that developed our new employment system, which resulted in a significant reduction of the complaints I mentioned earlier.

Team Meetings

The leadership team, which includes the senior directors, the director of compensation and HR information systems, and each of the divisional directors, meets biweekly. I meet with each member individually on at least a monthly basis and more frequently as needed. I also meet with the senior director for human services on a weekly basis because his division is so large and has so many pieces.

The entire HR organization consists of about 175 people. I plan quarterly meetings with the HR professionals throughout the university, including the support staff. We hold an annual HR conference on development opportunities for two days. The conference is a joint effort with the health system and includes workshops and guest speakers.

We have a newsletter called *HR Today* that is published five times during the academic year. There is an online edition as well as a hard copy that focuses on news and information. The newsletter gives us an opportunity to highlight employees or groups throughout the university. We also have a newsletter for retirees.

We communicate with employees about total compensation through another online newsletter. This publication focuses on salary and benefits, and if something important is coming up, we focus on specific initiatives.

Golden Rules

The golden rule for creating and maintaining a successful HR team is making sure employees understand the organization's values. As people come into the organization, I meet with them as soon as possible to review our values.

I have a list of ten behaviors that are valued in HR. The ten behaviors focus on what is valued in our HR organization: using good judgment, assessing priorities and using time wisely, using effective personal techniques to influence decisions, understanding that there is more than one way to accomplish any goal, knowing that what's good today may not be good tomorrow, demonstrating an expansion of technical knowledge and skills, showing care and concern for the well-being of the team, continuously improving behaviors, initiating change to assure quality products that meet customers' needs and requirements, communicating as a shared responsibility, sharing responsibility for personal growth and development, and demonstrating our knowledge of and sensitivity to the goals of our customers.

Everybody has a copy of our value statement. It helps people get off on the right foot and understand what is expected of them. There is an eleventh value I have talked about with every employee. I want people to know how important it is that we precisely and specifically measure our contributions while recognizing that we don't always have the information we need in order to do so.

Our values are the foundation of our team. We meet with people on a regular basis and make sure they're involved in substantive decision-making. We want employees to understand that even when we don't agree, it is important for them to understand why we decided to take a specific action. We believe in making sure everyone has the information and resources they need to do their jobs.

Charlene Moore Hayes became vice president for human resources at The Johns Hopkins University in November of 2003 after serving for nearly twenty years as a human resources professional elsewhere.

Ms. Hayes had been North Carolina State's associate vice chancellor for human resources, the university's chief human resources officer, since January of 2000. She previously worked for nine years at Purdue University, where she held a series of increasingly responsible positions before becoming director of personnel services, the university's chief personnel officer. She began her human resources career in 1984 as a labor/employee relations specialist in Maryland's Montgomery County government and got her start in higher education with the University of California at San Diego.

Ms. Hayes's priorities include continuing to promote the university's initiatives on institutional diversity, making improvements to the university's compensation and benefits programs, and contributing to the effort of the Johns Hopkins Institutions—the university and health system together—to design and execute HopkinsOne, an enterprise-wide business systems project, including the development and implementation of a shared service center for human resource transactions.

Ms. Hayes grew up in Holly Springs, Mississippi. A 1978 graduate of Cornell University where she majored in Africana studies, she earned a law degree in 1984 from George Washington University. She has led workshops and has been a speaker on a variety of human resource topics at regional and national conferences for the College and

University Professional Association for Human Resources and the National Association of College and University Attorneys. Ms. Hayes has focused her volunteer efforts on programs that benefit youth. She and her husband, Floyd W. Hayes III, have one daughter, Kia. Ms. Hayes has three stepchildren and three grandchildren from her husband's previous marriage.

Dedication: *To my husband, Floyd W. Hayes III, for all of his support. To my friend and colleague, Colleen Crooker, for her inspiration. To my daughter, Kia.*

Managing Compensation and Benefits

Robert J. Haertel

Senior Vice President, Compensation and Benefits

Assurant Inc.

Simply stated, my management style is this: I listen, ask, discuss, and then act. And this is the style I encourage in my work group.

Compensation and benefits cross all organizational lines and levels in the workplace. Consequently, it is critical that people in this area understand their company's business model, including both the jobs and the products. Although compensation and benefits is often looked at as a quantitative function, the core of the function needs to be developed from a human resources (HR) perspective. That is to say, as part of the HR function, compensation and benefits professionals provide a service and need to be attuned to the dynamics of their client groups within the company. I try to foster that awareness with my work group as well as with my colleagues and client groups. The design and administration of compensation and benefits programs are the products we deliver. As a team, we need to ensure that we are providing our clients with cost-effective products delivered in an efficient fashion.

At the outset, it is important to emphasize that compensation should be discussed in terms of total compensation. What a person earns includes more than the paycheck; compensation also includes bonuses, benefits, training, and development, as well as the overall work environment. It is the responsibility of the compensation and benefits group to consider all the components of the compensation package in determining plan design and reward programs. Some rewards are clearly compensation-related, while others can be categorized as benefits. Increasingly, plans cross both areas. That is why I will frequently refer to compensation and benefits as equal components in the total rewards equation.

One underlying objective of all the programs we develop and administer is that they are designed to reward participants for successful performance. Once an employee understands the mechanics of his or her pay plan, they can work more effectively to deliver the desired results and optimize their pay. I think it is critical for each individual working in the compensation and benefits group to be well-versed in how our pay programs work. To reach that goal, each member of the compensation and benefits group needs to understand the pay plans and then, in turn, actively educate employees. Communication is key, and the compensation and benefits group should be keenly aware of their role as communicators.

Participants in pay plans, which basically covers every employee from entry level to the chief executive officer, should understand how and why they are paid. Sometimes, the relationship between pay and performance is clear, such as when a salesperson is rewarded for making a sale. At other times, the relationships between pay and performance are more circuitous and may need to be clarified. For example, incentive pay or bonuses for staff positions are typically tied to project deliverables or quality measures. Unless the relationship between expected results and the bonus amount is clearly described, the participant may not appreciate the connection. This is called the "line of sight" between the results someone is working toward and the actual compensation. It is important that everyone, including compensation and benefits plan administrators, managers, and employees, understand the relationship between pay and performance. They should be comfortable that the pay system is fair and equitable. The ideal situation is for participants and administrators to be well-versed in the plan mechanics and then to become cheerleaders and promote the process.

Qualities of a Successful Team

The single greatest quality about the people in my work group is that they care about their work. They act with professionalism and take personal pride and interest in the quality of their work.

Professionals in compensation and benefits have several functional areas they have to thoroughly understand. What makes my group effective is that they go beyond the technical part of their jobs and also understand how the compensation and benefits model fits in the business model. They do not just look at pay. When they work on a compensation plan, they go beyond the equations and analyze how the plan will align with the business strategy and goals. They look at how the plan will be accounted for in the financial reports. They research what legal issues relate to the plan, and considerable effort is spent developing communication materials that are effective and easy to understand. My group understands that developing compensation and benefits plans involves balancing many factors.

For example, recent legislative changes have dramatically altered how compensation plans can be designed and administered. The American Jobs Creation Act completely changed the compensation landscape two years ago. This new law forced everyone in this profession to rethink almost everything they had previously learned about compensation and benefits. The law needed to be understood and then implemented in the design of our pay programs. Then, going beyond the design issues, these changes had to be communicated to participants. They analyzed the law and researched how it applied to our programs. After this work was done, they recommended the appropriate changes to our plans. Those efforts, to me, demonstrated that my work group's professional standards were—and continue to be—incredibly high.

Communication is critical to the effectiveness of compensation and benefits programs. This point cannot be overemphasized. The ultimate effectiveness of our compensation and benefits group was tied to how they actively got involved in understanding the new legislation.

Another dramatic change in the area of compensation involved recent accounting rules, although there are many who say these rules are always changing. For example, recent accounting rules changed how equity—or stock-based plans—should be handled. The compensation and benefits group needed to understand the implication of these changes on our compensation programs.

Legal and accounting changes are just two recent examples of how the rules surrounding compensation and benefits are changing. Our success as a group requires that everyone be up to the task of continually learning new standards and then applying these new rules to our programs. On a purely practical level, if we did not have this level of expertise and commitment by the group, we would not be successful.

From a management perspective, I believe it is important to encourage continuous learning. This includes both formal education as well as collegial conversations. To this end, we conduct frequent sessions to discuss projects, reflect on recent legal or business developments, and generally share ideas.

For example, let's consider recent developments regarding 401(k) plans. In my group, we have several experts in the area of retirement plans. When recent tax changes were announced, I looked to our group to consider what the implications of the new rules might be for our plans. Specifically, a recent tax change permits companies to offer a Roth 401(k) feature, which is effectively similar to a Roth IRA that is available to many U.S. taxpayers. I looked to our internal experts to consider whether this change would be appropriate for our company. As part of this evaluation, we met as a group. The initial part of the discussion was educational (e.g., description of the new rules and examples) followed by a conversation about whether this new plan fit with our plan goals and philosophy.

Although this may sound hackneyed, our work group actually does encourage everyone to talk freely about what is going on in our profession. The group actively stays apprised of trends and developments though publications, conferences, and professional associations, and this information is openly discussed and shared. I am very happy to say we have very few work silos, and that is one characteristic that really contributes to making us effective as a work group.

The group I work with is extremely intelligent and motivated to stay up to date with what is going on in the company as well as anticipate legislative changes and business trends.

The Compensation and Benefits Team: Working Relationships

The key areas in my work team are benefits and compensation. In the benefits area, the work is divided into two disciplines: retirement and health and welfare. In the compensation area, the work falls under the following sections: executive compensation, compensation administration, compensation deferral plans, and equity plans. In each of these areas, we have daily one-on-one discussions, and as a team we meet at least every other week.

One of my goals within this work group is to keep people informed. Changes in any area may have significant effects in other groups. Project updates—whether good news or bad, whether successful results or project delays—are critical to keeping an operation moving in the right direction. My strategy is to keep all of the groups apprised of what is happening in the other areas. Many times, changes in one area may have a ripple effect throughout the compensation and benefits area. If strategies and objectives change in our business groups, these changes can affect different plans within our group.

My relationship with my team is participative. It is a very open model. I am a believer in identifying obstacles so they can be overcome. The goal is to work toward the desired results. Hopefully, there is no intimidation in my management approach.

One strategy I use is: "communicate early; communicate often." For example, if there is a potential that we will need to develop a new program, there are advantages to alerting the group of possible changes. If I start communicating the situation early, even if the change itself does not happen for another eighteen months, people are comfortable with the concept because we have taken the time to get familiar with the issues. It facilitates communications and acceptance if and when the need for the plan change arises. Additionally, this inclusionary approach gets people brainstorming about how the plan should be designed.

My office is in the same area as the workspace for my group. As such, I am part of the process; I am part of the conversations and ideas. Hopefully, this is an energizer for the work group. And while I can think of several reasons why it may not be a great idea to situate a group manager amidst the work group, in this instance I believe it facilitates the workflow. A key strength of my work group is its creativity. I believe my proximity to the work group cuts down delays between ideas and action. The communicative style we foster as a work group encourages the discussion and refinement of new approaches to problems.

When recruiting employees, I look for people who are willing to work as part of a team. Based upon experience, I believe that what works best is an environment that values results more than egos. When a team has everyone focused and cooperating, things get done. I look for people who are knowledgeable and willing to share that knowledge with others. The objective is to foster communications and teamwork. Information sharing is in fact a form of cross-training. I value a team's ability to influence others as opposed to getting things accomplished by brute force. While it is important to get things done, it is also important to get things done using the right process. The team cannot be destroyed for the sake of results.

Compensation and Benefits: Challenges

As I mentioned earlier, during the past eighteen months, the rules surrounding compensation have gone through dramatic changes, specifically as they relate to the law and accounting. Consequently, compensation groups have had to go to their business groups and effectively change the way the compensation river flows. Where the law allowed, some plans were grandfathered, meaning the existing plans could continue. However, new plans had to be designed, approved, implemented, and communicated. Generally speaking, working with senior management and HR professionals was straightforward. These groups understood the changing rules. The more significant challenge was communicating with participants as to why the rules were changing. The challenge was getting the information to the actual participants regarding compensation plans— those individuals whose paychecks ultimately would be affected. I recall that one model I used in designing communication plans was to ensure that the information and materials were clear enough that the participant would be able to take them home and accurately explain the changes to his or her spouse. Throughout the change process, it was important to remember that people's pay would be affected by the changes that were made. Acceptance of the compensation plans as well as the ultimate effectiveness of these changes was dependent to a large extent on how well the plan was communicated.

It is often said that to market a product, you need to be able to describe it effectively in the time it takes to ride in an elevator. With that in mind, it is difficult to distill the details of a compensation plan into a concise summary to fit into an elevator conversation. It can be difficult to encapsulate legal and accounting changes in a way everyone readily grasps and understands. When an employee's paycheck changes, that raises concern on several levels. Being able to address employee concerns on both the emotional and economic level is the challenge.

The trends and requirements in the workplace are continually changing. A few years ago, I was involved in a company going public. That change dramatically altered how compensation was being delivered. Most notably, our compensation approach was reshaped since the company suddenly had stock to use as a reward and incentive. The initial public offering also coincided with legislative changes as well as Internal Revenue Service and accounting updates. Regulations were changing in light of the American Jobs Creation Act and Sarbanes-Oxley. Understanding these changes was the first requirement. The next step was to align our compensation programs with these new rules. Finally, we needed to align our compensation plans with the business strategy. And all the while the compensation plans were being updated, the challenge to solve was: how do we communicate these plan changes to participants?

Obviously, communication strategies differ depending on the size of the audience. If the audience is a small, contained group, more personal question-and-answer sessions are a viable option. However, sometimes changes take place on a large scale. Communicating compensation plan changes that affect thousands of people can be a daunting undertaking. We have made a few steps in the right direction, but we are always looking for ways to improve.

One of our new strategies for communicating changes is the use of Webcasts. Participants via the Internet can log on for a live presentation and send instant message questions to the facilitator. An advantage is that participants can join the presentation from their home or office. Additionally, this broadcast maintains confidentiality because participants do not know who else is logged into the session. Finally, when it comes to questions, since participants cannot see who is logged on, they are less apprehensive about asking a question. When questions come in via the instant message feature, the answers are either incorporated into the presentation or read aloud and answered specifically. In either case, there is no need to identify who is asking the question.

As another communication tool, we use a Web site to store compensation plan materials and forms for employees. With this approach, participants can access plan information or forms when they need them.

Robert J. Haertel is senior vice president of Assurant Inc., a premier provider of specialized insurance products and related services in North America and selected other markets. He is responsible for the corporate compensation and benefits departments.

Mr. Haertel began his career in human resources as an employee relations generalist for Shell Oil Company. He then went on to hold various human resources positions specializing in compensation and human resources technology at Citicorp, Engelhard Corporation, and CS First Boston.

Mr. Haertel received a B.A. from Providence College and an M.A. from Rice University.

Mr. Haertel is a certified compensation professional and a member of World at Work (formerly the American Compensation Association) and the Society of Human Resources Management.

Actions Really Do Speak Louder than Words

Terri A. Lowell

Former Vice President, Human Resources and Development

Glazer's Family of Companies

Creating a Vision

One of the most important competencies a human resources (HR) leader brings to the table is the ability to create a vision for HR. Over the years, one of the skills I've refined is the ability to do exactly that—create a vision for the HR team I am leading and communicate it in a way that engenders excitement and commitment. As a senior HR executive, I have two fundamental beliefs. First, I believe people come to work wanting to do a good job. Second, I believe the HR function—appropriately designed, organized, and executed—can make a positive difference in people's lives. In the past several years, I've had the unique opportunity to be able to build a number of HR functions from the ground up. Both the vision I create and the HR talent I bring to the team must support these two fundamental beliefs.

As a first step, I begin to create the HR vision by doing a lot of listening. I spend significant amounts of time in the field and at headquarters listening to people at all levels and in various functions. My goal is to understand what they enjoy and don't enjoy about their jobs and the company. From their perspective, I want to know what is working and what isn't. If there is one universal truth about work that I believe in strongly, it's that we all want our company to be a great place to work. My challenge is to figure out what HR can do to create or sustain a great working environment. Secondly, I systematically analyze all HR levers that contribute to a company's financial performance and organizational health. This time for analysis and reflection is critically important, and in my experience, it's often a low priority on a busy HR executive's agenda. I force myself to take the time to reflect on key questions such as: "Do our compensation and incentive practices drive the right kind of behaviors?" "Does the organization bring in the best talent it can afford?" "Is there a strong leadership bench?" "Does the organization value a diversity of people, styles, and work approaches?" "What performance metrics is HR using now, and what should these measurements be going forward?" "What do our internal customers say about the quality of HR service they receive?" What skills and competencies will our employees need five years from now?" "Ten years from now?" "What stories will be told about our corporate culture?"

The HR vision I develop will honor the past and the efforts of those who contributed to past successes, but it will create new possibilities for even better organizational performance. Finally, I communicate, communicate, communicate. In small groups, large groups, and one on one, I share the vision I have for HR within the company's HR community and with the company's leaders and associates. My goal is to create excitement and passion for the HR vision and change agenda that energizes the team and removes any preconceived beliefs of what they thought was possible. Change is possible, and together as a team, we can do it.

Developing the HR Strategy and Work Plan

It's essential that the HR strategy and work plan are aligned with the company's business strategy and operating plan. Additionally, the HR strategy should appropriately match the business situation. For example, the HR strategy in a start-up or turnaround situation will be very different from a sustaining situation. There will be noticeable differences in terms of time pressures, decision-making, resource requirements, and need for organizational change that the HR strategy and work plan must account for. To be successful, an HR leader needs to correctly and quickly diagnose the business situation.

In terms of key relationships, I've found that building strong partnerships with the chief executive officer, chief financial officer, vice president of operations, vice president of sales and marketing, and vice president of strategy expedites learning and, ultimately, the development of the HR strategy and work plan. These partnerships also offer business partners the opportunity to poke holes in the HR strategy. This group is a great test market for pre-selling and getting feedback. They will also play a critical role in visibly supporting the HR strategy throughout the organization, so it's important to build coalitions early on in the process. In the strategy implementation phase, it's important that HR serves as a barometer that accurately measures the pressure caused by organizational change. In my experience, the most difficult aspect of HR strategy implementation is determining how much disruption the organization can absorb. If there is too much disruption, business operations could be adversely affected, and the HR agenda may be suspended or stopped altogether. If there's too little disruption (i.e., no visible changes seen by the organization), there is a real risk that the HR strategy will be seen as a "flavor of the month" and be dismissed by the organization. It's a delicate balance that should be continuously monitored through open dialogue in meetings and one-on-one conversations as well as pulse surveys and so on.

Building the HR Team

In the past several years, I've had the opportunity to build an HR team from the ground up (a start-up) and mold a team I inherited to perform at a higher level and accomplish HR work they had never done before (a realignment). Both of these business situations required different approaches to building the HR team.

In the start-up situation, I had very limited resources, so my first challenge was to identify talent to fill key roles in the department. The HR career opportunities were easy to sell because we were all energized by the business and its possibilities. The risk in this type of situation was hiring too quickly because we were desperate for resources. I interviewed and hired the first few team members who then joined me in the selection process for other key HR roles. As a testimony to the initial team's commitment (and endurance), we decided to take whatever time was necessary to get the right people in the right positions. If this meant each of us had to work longer hours, we were willing to do so because, ultimately, the team would benefit by bringing the right talent on board. Our results were impressive. We had only one individual leave the team in the start-up phase, which represented about a 7 percent attrition rate.

In the realignment situation, I needed to assess the capabilities of the HR team I had inherited with the understanding that (1) the company had made no real investment in HR in the past decade and (2) the company's view of the HR function was quite antiquated. I was an outsider coming in to make changes, and not everyone wanted change or thought it was even necessary. My approach in this situation was to assess the existing HR team's technical expertise, their judgment, the quality of their relationships in the organization, and their openness and willingness to change. I also made a point of not criticizing existing team members or the work they had done. Instead, I asked a lot of questions and I listened. Over time, I learned that any previous gaps in HR service delivery were due to the team being under-resourced rather than under-skilled. As part of the HR strategy, I developed a staffing plan I shared with the existing team. They provided input and participated in the interviewing process for new team members. Both existing and new team members came together beautifully and, as a team, we changed the reputation and performance of the HR function for the better.

Creating a Positive Team Environment

With every HR team I've led, I've tried to build a work environment where walls or silos around HR functional areas such as employee relations, compensation and benefits, recruiting, and so on, do not exist. My expectation is that every member of the team understands the HR vision and strategy and buys into the fact that we succeed as a team—not as individuals. Our goal as a team is to proactively anticipate business needs, design HR solutions to meet those needs, and then flawlessly execute. It's also important to me that members of the HR team implicitly trust one another to act in the best interests of the team, the people we serve, and the business. With a strong grounding in trust and respect among HR team members, I've found that we've been able to accomplish what others thought was not possible.

As an HR leader, I also want to create an environment where team members enjoy coming to work every day. We invest so much of our lives in our careers that I've learned how important it is to work with people you enjoy. I make a point of getting to know the team not just as the great HR professionals they are, but also as the individual persons they are—and I encourage everyone to do the same. I've found that this creates a unique bond that will remain strong through the ups and downs we experience in business cycles.

Personal Management Style

In my first vice president of HR assignment, I initially managed the team exactly how I liked to be managed. I wanted my manager to provide me with basic information, let me figure out the opportunities, and be available for questions and brainstorming. I quickly learned that what worked well for me and my direct manager didn't necessarily work well for the people who reported to me. Fortunately, I participated in a 360-degree leadership development process early on in my tenure and got some terrific feedback from the team on what I did well and what I needed to do differently. Six months into this assignment, I was able to adjust my style to better serve the individual needs of team members. The 360-degree feedback I received resulted in a number of "ah-has" for me, and I consider it to have been a defining moment in my development as an HR leader.

In terms of my personal management style, I have high expectations for performance for myself and the HR team. I set challenging goals and expect team members to achieve them. Most importantly, I sincerely believe we can achieve them. My goal is to consistently demonstrate the optimism and confidence I have in our team's capability so it's transferred and internalized by others. I work with an intensity and focus that is palpable. I expect HR team members to do the same. That being said, I prefer to work in a supportive environment, so I manage using a positive and supportive approach to bring out the best in others. I genuinely appreciate the efforts and contributions made by individuals on the team. I celebrate successes and openly discuss mistakes or challenges so we can learn from them. I encourage team members to try new ideas and approaches. "Not invented here" has never resonated with me. I enjoy seeing the HR team's creativity as they solve business issues. I also realized long ago that no leader is perfect, including me. This realization is very freeing and has allowed me to be vulnerable with the team. I admit mistakes when I make them, and I self-correct. I don't lose sleep over mistakes anymore; I move on and ensure that I've learned from them. When a team member makes a mistake, I manage using this same personal philosophy. I listen, provide coaching or whatever is necessary to correct the mistake, and I encourage them to learn and keep moving forward.

Essential Team Characteristics

Members of the HR team need to be results-oriented and competent within their area of expertise. I value strong intellectual capability appropriately balanced with organizational savvy. In terms of interpersonal style, I look for enthusiasm, energy, emotional maturity, authenticity, and depending upon the business situation, endurance. Regardless of whether team members tend to be extroverts or introverts, they need to openly communicate with me and with each other. There should be no hidden agendas or sacred cows. Our communication as a team should be in the spirit of full disclosure wherever possible. Whether the team members are compensation, organizational development, or training professionals, they should be able to think strategically, creatively, and demonstrate technical expertise in their given areas of expertise. I also want them to be comfortable working independently, and I've found that this level of comfort develops over time. I want team members to take the expertise they have and drive their own agendas. I trust them to be able to apply what they know to improve organizational performance.

On-Boarding Essentials

It's important to develop a structured learning or on-boarding plan for new team members prior to their joining the team. In fact, I've found it very helpful in the recruiting process to be able to show prospective team members how their first thirty days, ninety days, or six months on the job will look. The on-boarding process is intended to accelerate the new hire's start in two key areas: learning the business and building key relationships. The success of the on-boarding process is a joint accountability for me and the new team member. The plan is designed so each day out in the market, each meeting, and so on, has a distinct learning point. I meet weekly with the new team member to evaluate how the process is working, and if we need to make any adjustments, we do so in real time. It's particularly important for HR professionals to spend sufficient time in the field to gain a deep understanding of the business and its customers, consumers, strengths, opportunities, and so on. This helps them build credibility more quickly and expedites their contribution to the team and the business.

As an example, I recently hired a recruiting manager to lead efforts to improve our success in attracting and retaining sales associates across the organization. With the support of the company president, our recruiting manager spent his first ninety days working every aspect of the sales associate position. He shadowed district managers and called on customers. He took orders, threw cases, built displays, merchandised stores, made deliveries, worked the will-call window on a Friday, and so on. In his first two weeks on the job, he lost twelve pounds and understood the incredible opportunities the position offered as well as its mental and physical demands. At the conclusion of his ninety-day "in-market" experience, he came to corporate with an intimate understanding of one of the company's most critical roles and began to immediately revise our approach to selecting talent. Today, he is an incredible advocate for the sales associate position and can speak with authenticity about the good, the bad, and the ugly of the role. Already, we have seen significant improvement in the caliber of talent hired, and that improvement has translated into increased sales for this particular group of new sales associates.

Key Team Players

In building an HR function, it's important to have strong expertise in functional areas such as compensation and benefits, recruiting, employee relations, training, and organizational development. Additionally, I've found it to be extremely beneficial to have a team member who can serve as HR's project management office. This is particularly important when an HR system implementation is required. I am conservative with head count requests and carefully analyze each required role to determine if it's sustainable over time or can be filled using external consulting resources. To ensure that the HR change agenda is established at the grassroots level, I leverage the HR generalist role. The HR generalist is assigned to the field and is co-located with key clients (e.g., a business unit president and his or her direct reports). They facilitate the delivery of the HR strategy and work plan by serving as a strategic partner, change agent, functional/administrative expert, and employee champion for their assigned client group.[1] In organizations more familiar with the traditional reactive and administrative role of HR, this HR generalist role will quickly demonstrate the strategic value HR can add to the business. I stay out of the way and let the HR generalist become an integral part of the client team. Selecting the right talent to fill this particular role is one of the most important decisions I will make in building the HR team.

Staying Connected

I use a variety of approaches to stay connected, and I'm very flexible making changes based on feedback from the team. As the team is getting established, I hold weekly staff meetings with planned agendas. I rotate responsibility for facilitating the staff meetings among team members so everyone gets experience pulling them together. The single objective of our staff meetings is to move the HR work plan forward. It's important to

---

[1] Reference to the changing nature of HR described by Dave Ulrich in his book, *Human Resource Champions*.

everyone that staff meetings are not just an information dump. We raise issues, share information that pertains to all, make decisions, and determine next actions as an outcome of these meetings. As we learn to work together as a team, we'll change the frequency of our meetings to biweekly or even monthly as appropriate. I also meet regularly one on one with team members. Depending on the individual and the initiatives he or she is working on, these one-on-ones may occur weekly or biweekly. This is an opportunity for a detailed update on progress to date, and it ensures that there's adequate communication, feedback, and, ultimately, no surprises. In the past, I've also held HR off-sites when there's been a need to plan a new initiative or develop next year's HR agenda. I will generally include a team learning opportunity as part of the off-site. I am an avid user of e-mail and voicemail, which I also use to stay connected with the HR team.

Working with the Executive Team

In my past few assignments, I've joined the executive team as an outsider coming in with particular expertise the organization wanted to invest in. In both instances, there was a strong desire on the part of the chief executive officer and president for HR to serve a critical change agent role and "bring HR into the twenty-first century." Interestingly, while their messages were the same, their behaviors were very different.

In Company A, the chief executive officer and president visibly supported the HR strategy, invested in resources, and publicly spoke to why the HR strategy and investment in HR were key to the business's long-term success. This consistent and visible support facilitated my ability to build relationships with the executive team members and, over time, introduce successful change initiatives.

In Company B, the chief executive officer's and president's messages were identical to those of Company A. However, when the first arrows were shot regarding (1) increased overhead allocation and (2) a third-party ethics hotline being a bad idea, they disappeared. This sent a mixed message to the executive team and other leaders about the senior-level commitment to HR and change. The change journey was compromised, and challenges continue even today.

I learned and grew a lot through both experiences. First, I learned how critical it is to assess authenticity and readiness for change when interviewing with C-level executives. Secondly, I learned that just because a chief executive officer and president say they want change, it doesn't mean the organization will accept it absent their ongoing support, frequent communication, and willingness to hold leaders accountable.

Useful Advice

The best piece of advice I ever received was to focus on the behaviors people exhibit and not put too much emphasis on their words. I believe the old adage is: "Actions speak louder than words." When I've been smart enough to heed this advice, I've accurately predicted the outcomes of business challenges or employee situations.

Terri A. Lowell has extensive experience leading human resources teams in start-up and turnaround environments. Most recently, she was vice president of human resources and development at Glazer's Family of Companies, a privately held company that is currently the second-largest distributor of beverage alcohol in the United States.

Ms. Lowell has more than twenty years of human resources experience. Prior to joining Glazer's, she held the position of director of organizational capability and diversity at Frito-Lay North America. She has held other leadership positions at eLoyalty, where she was vice president of employee loyalty, and at Goldman, Sachs & Co., where she was vice president of human resources. She began her human resources career at BP-Amoco.

Ms. Lowell has an M.B.A. from Northwestern University's Kellogg Graduate School of Management, an M.A. in teaching English as a second language from the University of Illinois, and a B.A. in Spanish from the University of Delaware. She and her husband, Don Skillern, live in Dallas, Texas.

Dedication: *To the outstanding human resources professionals who partnered with me at Goldman, Sachs & Co., eLoyalty, PepsiCo, and Glazer's. I sincerely thank you for your commitment to excellence, your willingness to go "above and beyond," and your heartfelt belief that human resources can make a difference.*

Successfully Executing Change

Steven J. Heaslip

Senior Vice President, Global Human Resources

International Flavors & Fragrances Inc.

Implementing a Vision

Implementing a vision is all about the future, and in order to achieve your vision, you must always be looking forward. For example, when I came to International Flavors & Fragrances Inc. in 2001, it was a traditional human resources (HR) philosophy and team. They were focused on administration and customer service to line management, as opposed to being focused on the business and on creating a positive environment for colleagues. In creating a vision for the future, one of my responsibilities has been to transform the HR team into people who understand the business and go beyond the superficial request to understand the business need. They need to have the confidence and inquisitiveness to try to discover what their business partner is trying to accomplish and potentially offer a different solution. For example, instead of the HR person trying to figure out a way to help a manager get a promotion for an employee, I encourage him or her to get beyond the first layer in order to reveal the true need of the business or business partner. It could be that the manager simply wants to recognize the employee for a job well done, in which case a solution with fewer organizational implications is preferable.

In moving toward this new vision, one must be patient and impatient at the same time. To accomplish this, I would characterize my management style as balanced, respectful, and considerate yet very direct. I hold high expectations of my employees and colleagues, but I recognize that you don't achieve a new vision overnight. Accordingly, you need to be selective in terms of choosing the issues you take a very tough stand on versus those you are willing to simply shape and guide. In my view, a manager needs to possess an understanding of all the angles and intuitively know which approach makes sense when.

Executing Change

Putting change into action requires clarity and tenacity. You need to be very clear, and repetitively so, about what changes are required. You need to give people the opportunity to change. And if change doesn't happen, you need to take the opportunity to change people. This is not something someone can be sent to a course for. We have to imprint our vision upon our team and then support them in every way we are able. In the early days of change, it is not uncommon to find people who don't really believe it is real, even if they agree with it. When I first came to International Flavors & Fragrances Inc., it was very rare to find an HR person challenging a line manager or offering up a solution that was different from what had been requested. Even after I made it clear what was expected, they were still reluctant to challenge. However, I needed to let them know they had my support and an ability to go back and challenge in a way that would not get their legs cut out from under them.

I believe managing an HR team is much more complex compared with managing other functions such as sales, marketing, or operations. On any given issue, there are several competing needs. In HR, you have to consider the needs of the employees, the needs of the line manager involved, and the needs of the business (read as shareholders). These needs are not always aligned. Indeed, they are often not aligned—and the challenge is to find the solution that adequately addresses the most compelling needs. This is made even more complicated by the fact that HR does not have a lot of direct authority. As opposed to being in a decision-making position, we in HR must steer things along from a position of influence and guidance. That requires complex communication and negotiation skills.

Accordingly, in executing change throughout the HR team, it is not easy to distill the process down into specific skills. It is highly possibly that there may be two people who possess equivalent skill levels; however, one might be very successful and the other might be struggling. In this case, the difference is in each person's ability to see the competing needs and arrive at the "sweet spot" in terms of a solution and in their way of dealing with people, communicating, and interjecting themselves into the business so as to deliver the best outcome.

What has made me successful in accomplishing this change relates to engaging my team and getting it committed to my vision. Another aspect of success is supporting my team. Finally, it is highly important to lead by example. I think my direct reports would tell you I spend a lot of time doing all of the above and constantly coaching and advising each of them.

Working as a Team

I have my group organized geographically, and again, they need to find a balance somewhere between both serving the needs of their geography (region) and understanding the needs of the whole team and the whole enterprise. This is particularly true when dealing with international compensation policies. A lot of people really don't understand international compensation, although they think they do. Compensation practices around the world are very diverse, and it would be foolhardy for me to put in certain elements of a compensation plan on a universal basis around the world. It would not mirror the markets in many geographies. At the same time, however, what must be consistent is that we pay our employees competitively no matter where in the world they work. By this means, the need for corporate consistency is balanced with the need to reflect local market practice.

My most successful regional HR heads understand the tension between global consistency and local customization and then respond to it properly. An imbalanced response will create inconsistencies that are detrimental to the enterprise as a whole or result in decisions that do not serve the local environment adequately, thereby being detrimental to the enterprise as a whole as well.

In order to be successful at this, we all need to be able to collaborate and maintain a strong will to perform well. In addition, it is important to be able to make tough decisions and be open to other ways of looking at a particular issue. I always tell my managers that working in a geographically diverse organization requires a high degree of sophisticated thinking among them.

Key Players on the HR Team

I have four regional vice presidents of HR who are responsible for Asia, India, Europe, and the Americas, respectively. I also have a global vice president of training and development and a global vice president for change management and HR consulting. In addition, I have a director of HR systems and administration as well as a director of global compensation and benefits. In all, I have nine direct reports.

I meet with my corporate staff every week or two. In terms of the regional managers, I talk with them regularly; however, in terms of meeting as a group, it varies based on what projects and activities are on the agenda. Typically, we meet two to three times a year for approximately four to five days.

During our last meeting, our objective was to review, rank, and evaluate all the management-level jobs in the organization. We also spent a fair amount of time looking at improvements for our incentive programs and analyzing international assignment policies with a view to generating cost savings.

In order to keep my team members motivated and aligned, I am dedicated to maintaining a fluid process of communication. While this results in keeping everyone on the same page, keeping them motivated is a different sort of challenge. They occupy senior roles, and they must be given the autonomy and responsibility to make decisions. That decision-making, in and of itself, is motivating to these team members. Having said that, particularly in an organization in which we are transforming the HR function, it is easy to forget about the progress we have made and to only focus on barriers and setbacks. When my team feels as if they are not making progress, in order to provide them with motivation, I remind them of the difference they have made as individuals over a relatively brief period of time. This is something they tend to respond very well to.

Regarding our rewards and recognition programs, as it relates to our more formalized programs, I do not hesitate to nominate my own people to participate. My top performers have found themselves in new, bigger, and more challenging roles. In fact, eight of my nine direct reports have been in position less than three years. I also believe, however, that simple verbal recognition and expressed appreciation go a long way.

Challenges

One of the largest challenges we face is cultural change. Business today is very difficult, and our industry is no exception. The market requires never-ending growth and profitability—yet customers demand more and better for less. How does one reconcile this in a company that has enjoyed a lot of past success in the absence of market or customer pressures? We must recognize that we are in a different environment today, and shift from a culture of entitlement into one of meritocracy that reflects the marketplace.

HR is on the front lines driving this transition. This will be accomplished in a number of phases. We have already examined our compensation plan and moved from a globally consistent approach (which is incorrect, resulting in some countries being above market versus other countries being below market) to one that is on market locally around the world. There is no more difficult thing to accomplish than to introduce a new compensation arrangement. And while this was not a popular move, it was one that was essential to the business.

Another phase of cultural change involves explicitly developing and cascading organizational values. This too is difficult, because as we all know, you can't just talk the talk—to really achieve a cultural shift, you must walk the walk.

As senior vice president of global human resources, Steven J. Heaslip is responsible for fully developing and implementing International Flavors & Fragrances Inc.'s human resources strategy, including training and development, compensation, stock ownership, and reward and recognition programs.

Prior to joining International Flavors & Fragrances Inc. in July of 2001, Mr. Heaslip spent more than twenty-one years managing human resources initiatives for a variety of multinational corporations. Mr. Heaslip began his career as a production supervisor for Lever Brothers in Toronto, Canada. After transitioning into human resources, he progressed through a variety of consumer products companies, serving most recently as global vice president of human resources for Elizabeth Arden.

His experience includes all aspects of human resources such as labor and employee relations, training, organizational development, compensation, benefits, and change management.

Mr. Heaslip holds a B.S. in chemistry from McMaster University.

Building Credibility
to Drive Success

Bill Ermatinger

Sector Vice President,

Human Resources and Administration

Northrop Grumman Corporation–Newport News

My Management Style

My management style is one of openness. My role is to work for my staff, not for my staff to work for me. I've been around a lot of leaders who felt their staff should work for them. My style is one of total collaboration.

I am always thinking about what I can do to make my team more successful. I want them to have the right tools, resources, communication, and strategy. I tell my team to live by the four Cs: credibility, collaboration, courage, and competence.

There's been a transformation in human resources (HR) over the past twenty years. Many HR executives used to think with a "cop mentality." My approach is to be a coach to business leaders, not a cop.

My Vision for the HR Team

I just joined Northrop Grumman's Newport News Sector a little more than a year ago. Northrop Grumman is currently made up of more than twenty major corporations that have been purchased in the past twelve years. I was part of the defense business of Westinghouse located in Maryland. Subsequently, Northrop Grumman purchased that operation in 1996. Just a few years ago, the company purchased Newport News Shipbuilding, which is where I am now. Newport News is the largest shipyard in the nation, employing 19,000 employees. This site is the United States' sole builder of nuclear aircraft carriers and shares nuclear submarine building duties with General Dynamics.

The culture here can be very rigid. At times, it has to be, given the type of material we have to work with. When you're a nuclear site, it's very important that everybody does A before they do B. We have to be regimented and controlled as it relates to our processes and procedures, and that mentality can very easily creep into our culture.

What I'm trying to take my HR team through is what I call the "four levels of HR." The first level is when management comes to HR with a problem, management informs HR what the solution is, and HR fails in executing that solution. If an HR team works at that level, it's not going to last very long. Level two is when management comes to HR with a problem, management still creates the solution, but this time HR executes the solution flawlessly. That's where a lot of the HR industry is today.

Level three is when management comes to HR with a problem but has no solution for their particular problem. HR has to figure out the solution and execute it flawlessly. For me, this is where strategic partnering starts to come into play. Unfortunately, some in the HR industry feel this is the highest level to obtain. Not true. The fourth level is when HR informs management of a pending problem, and then HR creates and executes a solution because HR knows the business as well as management does.

A lot of business executives like to play in the HR sandbox, but they're not always successful at it. I tell HR professionals that it's easier for us to understand how the business operates and play in their sandbox than for business leaders to try and understand our world. Besides, you want business leaders managing the business with little distractions.

To operate on this fourth level, we need business acumen and an understanding of profit and loss and the drivers of business. We have to understand financial metrics and know what drives the stock. It goes without saying that we also have to be experts in our area. If you cannot do the basics of HR (i.e., hire, fire, pay, benefits, etc.), no business leader will take you seriously.

Moreover, HR needs a continuous improvement mindset. We can't think we've found a solution that's going to be the end all, be all for the next twenty years. We have to be ethical and credible at all times, but we can't legislate morality. You have to walk the walk. Besides the chief executive officer, HR is the moral compass of an organization.

It is not enough that HR develops talent; we have to manage talent! At the fourth level, you will see business leaders come to HR with more than just HR issues. It's not enough to be requested to be at the table; we want to be demanded at the table. When I see a business leader canceling a meeting because their HR representative is going to be out of the office, I know I have people working at the fourth level.

Secrets to My Success

HR is not rocket science. The biggest thing that's helped me in my career is the concept of knowing the business challenges business leaders face or will face and creating HR solutions that will assist them. In addition, there is the ability to balance the business needs with the needs of its employees. Sometimes, those two conflict with each other, and there needs to be a balance.

I tell my HR professionals that "No" should never be the last word spoken to a customer. I'm okay with saying "No," but it's better to offer an alternative. Also, it is critical to explain the logic or reasoning behind a decision. Business leaders couldn't care less about a particular solution; they just want the problem fixed.

My Team

I have assigned an HR person to every division leader in the company. I want one person the leaders and workforce can go to. I don't care what kind of question they have; they should have one point of contact. My key players on my staff are my director of employment and operations, the director of compensation and benefits, the director of environmental health and safety, the director of learning and development, the director of labor relations, the director of security, and the director of community relations and ethics. (It sets a bad tone to have community relations and ethics too far down in the organization; it needs to be at the top.)

As a team, we meet every week. I meet with my team after the president meets with the executive staff, versus before. I hold my staff meetings a day after the president has his staff meeting, so I can tell my team members what they need to know. It's important that I get the information to them sooner rather than later.

Team Characteristics

We have created a competency model that has helped us greatly (see graph below). The model is made up of four complements. The first complement is personal credibility, the second complement is business acumen, the third complement is strategic contribution, and the fourth complement is HR expertise. Under each complement are numerous competencies. For example, personal credibility is made up of various competencies such as interpersonal savvy, effective communication, organizational agility, integrity and trust, results orientation, and emotional intelligence. We're trying to drive our model down into the HR organization, which will enable us to achieve fourth-level HR thinking.

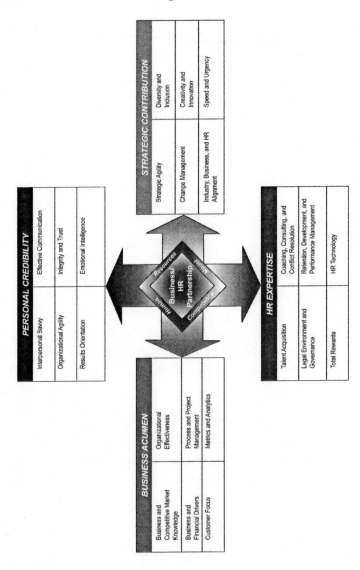

Typical Meetings

A hypothetical team meeting starts out with me reporting the business conditions that have changed since the last time we met. I always give people a framework. Even though each issue may not directly affect each person's job, it's important that everyone knows the complete puzzle so they can see how they fit into it.

After I give the team my report, they do the same in turn. We don't set goals; we have strategic meetings at off-sites. I require my staff to do everything as a team. I have a $25 million budget to control. In the old days, I gave the budgets to individual directors, and sure enough, every year something happened that I or they didn't anticipate, and we would have to make course corrections. Now they work the budget as a team; no more individual goals or metrics.

I decided to measure the team on one number—the total HR budget. I don't care if compensation overruns the budget. I'm not going to monitor it. All I care about is the overall amount. I let everyone manage that amount as a group. People trade off and work collaboratively. We even do bonuses, succession planning, merits, and job rotations as a team. Nothing is done behind closed doors.

My Relationship with the Chief Executive Officer

I've only been here about a year and a half. Since our chief executive officer held this job before I did, I don't have to spend much time explaining what is going on. A lot of HR people have to teach the chief executive officer HR. I don't have to do that.

My chief executive officer gives me his full support. I have a very strong relationship with him for just being here a short time. My office is right next to his, which is a positive statement to the workforce. We don't have a need for formal get-togethers because access is unlimited.

Best Advice

The best piece of advice I've ever received came from my father on the day I graduated from college. He told me to volunteer for everything nobody wants to do. He told me that at whatever job I have, I should look around at my co-workers, find a skill that is lacking, and obtain that skill.

Someone once asked me how you would know if you volunteered for too much. You know you've overextended yourself when you have to ask yourself if you're overextended.

The golden rule for creating a successful HR team is don't take yourself too seriously and give your team room to take risks. I tell people all the time that they need to relax and breathe. People are willing to take more risks when they realize they're not going to get killed. I always ask leaders when they last rewarded someone who took a risk and failed.

In order to be successful, you have to be credible. If you're not credible, no matter how good you are, you're not going to get anywhere. You also need courage. You need to push back on things that don't make sense and push forward on things that require active leadership.

Bill Ermatinger has been sector vice president of human resources and administration for Northrop Grumman Newport News since December of 2004. Newport News is the nation's sole designer, builder, and refueler of nuclear-powered carriers and one of only two companies capable of designing and building nuclear-powered submarines. Mr. Ermatinger's position has responsibility for human resources operations and employment; environmental, health, and safety issues; labor relations; community relations; security; equal employment opportunity and diversity; benefits; and employee services.

Prior to his current position, Mr. Ermatinger was director of employee relations for the Electronic Systems Sector in Baltimore, where he directed the day-to-day human resources and administration activities. He joined the company in 1987 as an associate human resources representative and held a number of human resources management positions with increasing responsibility in the areas of labor relations, employment law, compensation, and human resource generalist-related activities.

Developing and Managing a World-Class Human Resources Team

Jill Little

*Vice President, Americas Human Resources
and Organization*

Ericsson Inc.

Personal Management Style

Ericsson Inc. is a Swedish company; therefore, the Scandinavian management style greatly influences us here in the U.S. culture. Swedish management style conveys cultural norms, behaviors, and values. In order to be successful in Ericsson, you must be able to navigate in the American and Swedish styles.

On the American side, there is a participative and empowering leadership style that emphasizes teamwork, delegation of responsibility and authority, and an energizing spirited challenge to always exceed expectations and performance goals. On the Swedish side, you must understand "Jante law" and "lagom."

Jante law is a cultural code in Scandinavian countries that means: "You should not believe or show that you are better or more superior to anyone else." Jante law stresses the importance of the team, which faces the rewards or blame together. In telecommunications, where huge, complex research and development projects are the norm, this characteristic has proven to be a huge advantage for Ericsson.

Lagom means "just enough or the perfect amount." The Swedish national character is very much one of moderation and one to avoid extremes and conflicts on issues. However, also ingrained in this concept is that the solution to a situation or problem should be maximized or optimal.

The American-Swedish management style is, therefore, one that is consensus-driven on selected issues, strives for maximizing individual and organizational capabilities and solutions, and is very Ericsson values-driven: perseverance, respect, and professionalism.

The nature and complexity of Ericsson's business and products in a highly matrixed organization demands superb execution and constant teamwork.

A Vision for Managing Our HR Team

Our vision for human resources (HR) is to build organizational and individual capabilities in order to maximize company and employee performance. In addition, our vision for global HR is to continue to attract and develop high-performing, competent, and motivated individuals by building on everyone's competence and ambition to succeed in an exciting, diverse, and challenging environment.

I believe every person is a "different book." All individuals are not motivated in the same manner. Therefore, a good manager knows how to get the best out of people by developing an individual's capabilities. By developing the interests and capabilities of that person and aligning him or her with the company's business goals, an individual may add greater value to the company.

For example, one person may want the opportunity to be on a team to recruit at the university he or she graduated from. Maybe he or she has never even recruited before, but this opportunity would give him or her a chance to gain recruitment knowledge while visiting his or her alma mater. This provides the freedom to both invent and create new strategies for recruitment by throwing an individual into the mix due to the fact that he or she does not have a recruitment background. I like to challenge people by taking them out of their comfort zones.

For my direct reports, I would assess competence as well as the individual's interests and try to make it fun as well as a learning experience. In addition, I would establish a plan that includes education, skills, and resources and then establish a mentorship, which is one of the most effective ways to develop HR leadership.

Managing Your Team

With co-workers in the U.S. market, a local approach is taken, not a regional approach. Over five years, I have built a world-class regional HR team in more than thirty countries within the Americas. When I began, the HR function was completely in a silo by country. Some of the benefits of working in a team and in a highly collaborative manner are:

- Sharing of resources
- Centers of excellence
- In-sourcing of HR resources to take operational efficiency
- Competence transference

- International development opportunities
- Building up group trust and credibility to leverage influence in the business
- Shared training functions
- Shared benchmark practices
- Shared services centers
- Moving talent globally

This vision encourages innovation, experimentation, and development. The strategic focus is on developing leaders who can solicit ideas from individuals, the market, and customers and who can use team knowledge to make sound business decisions. The vision is people-caring and people-driven. There can be no company success without engaged, competent, and committed people.

Our Swedish chief executive officer, Carl-Henric Svanberg, believes that culture will defeat strategy every time. We are nurturing and developmental. Non-performers do get managed out if they cannot be coached up to high standards of performance; this is done in a very respectful way. We present an opportunity to help Ericsson, and our employees become more effective and productive in a very multicultural environment.

Past Management Successes

My successes are based on the ability to understand and use organization and individual behaviors, values, and culture to increase business results. It takes an entrepreneurial personality and an ability to develop and communicate the strategies and direction for HR with the team to build the types of relationships one needs to succeed. In addition, one must find a way to ensure that employees are committed and engaged to the tasks, and that we as a company are providing strong developmental and mentorship orientations. Some of my most prominent successes were the result of maximizing team performance by setting high standards—both ethically and professionally—and maintaining the ability to adapt and thrive on positive change.

Team Success

The success of the team is from within and has synergy. The team's results are greater than anything an individual member can do by himself or herself. The strengths of each member should be used, and we should take an efficient approach to managing in which the good of the team takes precedent over the good of one individual. Each person should have mutual respect and knowledge of each other's skills and competencies while being committed to each other's personal success, development, and growth.

In addition, each team member should view himself or herself as a role model for the company while reflecting the company's values and striving to achieve the goals in the most efficient manner. The team's success is weighted on its capacity to understand the HR vision and how the team fits into helping achieve company goals.

When I started out as an entry-level recruiter many years ago, my boss instructed me to not hire anyone I would not invite home to dinner as a friend. Therefore, a member of our team must possess high standards, values, and ethics, as well as be motivated to learn new skills and take on challenging tasks. Also, before we make a hire, we look for a person who is extremely competent, optimistic, driven for success, and who has a lot of positive energy. Lastly, we hope to bring in a new employee who possesses a desirable balance of intellect and stability, but who is also innovative.

It is also a good idea to have your HR team interview any potential new members who will come into the team. In this manner, everyone can accept the responsibility for mentoring and developing the new team member.

According to the Meyers-Briggs model, I have a diverse HR staff. I feel that difference is strength. Many new ideas do not usually come out of a homogeneous group.

Commitment to diversity is part of our drive to excellence in all areas of our business. Ericsson strives to make sure our commitment to diversity is reflected in the actions and behaviors of all employees. Diversity is related to our company's vision, values, behaviors, and ways of working.

Creating an Effective Work Environment

First, HR should be put at the heart of business strategies. By this I mean the work environment should reflect the values, principles, people commitment, and operational excellence of the company's culture. The employee/employer relationship is developed and a mutual respect occurs if communication is open, professional, respectful, and participative.

The work environment supports and empowers an individual. Motivation and morale can be increased by offering items such as flex hours, proper tools to do the job, challenging and satisfying work, training and development opportunities, proper pay and benefits, a good physical environment, and rewards systems. If HR is placed at the heart of the business strategies, employees will internalize a high standard of Ericsson's ways of working, thinking, and behaving.

The results will be increased productivity and performance. There will be less absenteeism, fewer employee relations issues, and in general, a happier and more productive employee.

The Biggest Challenges an HR Team Faces

Since my team is spread throughout thirty countries, we have the issue of how to work together virtually. Learning how to manage people at a distance using technology such as Web meetings, online chat, e-mail, and videoconferences is a challenge. But one cannot deny the future has arrived. There will be more and more virtual teams instead of the traditional traveling to a location to have face-to-face contact. Of course, one benefit of this is reduced travel expenses for the company. I have learned that unless the company is willing to invest in technology and virtual team training, virtual teams could be high in risk, especially if operating in different cultures.

I would venture to say that for global companies, the old model of team management followed by most companies is not sustainable. Virtual teams are the new way of working. As Ericsson is the leading wireless telecom company in the world, think wireless. You can be available anywhere and any time. Wireless technology will give you a clear competitive advantage and is critical to spreading corporate policies, messages, goals, and business strategies.

Goals for the Regional Team and Overcoming Cultural Barriers

Every year, Ericsson conducts a strategic planning session of the top 250 managers. The business goals that are prioritized during this session are rolled out globally. The management teams of each business unit, market unit, product unit, research and development unit, and so on, develop their plans to align with the overall business strategy of Ericsson. I take my key HR staff off site for a several-day session. Together, we develop the HR goals, metrics, and strategy to align with our global and local business goals. This year, we decided to convey these goals, objectives, key performance indicators, and metrics to the general HR population—during our quarterly group meeting—through a "Who Wants to Be a Millionaire?" format. After the goals were identified in this quiz, HR groups were broken up to work together to develop the implementation plans and assign responsibilities. The team had great fun but at the same time assimilated the HR strategic plan.

Working in a multicultural environment can be very challenging. I believe it is very much a learning and educational process. You should train a multicultural staff on the following process. First, one must approach any issue with an open mind and be open to listening to ideas or practices that may be opposite to what someone has been inculcated with for years. No judgment should be taken, and a two-way conversation to educate both parties on the subject under discussion should be facilitated. Lastly, a negotiation and support to a point of view acceptable by both parties can be finalized.

Measuring the Team's Success: Capitalizing on the Strengths of Your Employees

We are driven by a global performance management system and quantifiable metrics on the scorecard, which we review on a quarterly basis, making it easier to measure success. Each person also has his or her own individual performance goals and metrics and development plan. This helps reinforce and align to scorecard items.

However, it is not so easy to measure softer goals such as cultural change regarding our ways of leading. Still, the results will show up in our annual "employee dialogue survey," as we do have questions regarding cultural change. But as you know, true cultural change may take a period of years, not one performance review cycle. Therefore, milestones would be built into the implementation plan on the scorecard item if the goal would take more than one year.

It is important to have the team set up performance standards that stretch them but that are also attainable. One must prioritize and weigh how important each goal will be and what the impact will be to the customer, organization, or function. It is also key to ensure that there is a numeric measurement or a description of how to measure performance standards, as well as an effective way to track performance.

In order to capitalize on the strengths of our employees, I dedicate the time to find out the strengths and weaknesses of each member of my team. This inquiry is done by one-on-one conversations, competence assessment, projects I assign, and a 360-degree feedback tool.

I design into the annual development plan training to help fill gaps. The secret though is not to concentrate on the weaknesses, many of which you may never be able to really eliminate, but to concentrate on helping an individual leverage and develop their strengths. I believe each person is a different book and that each brings special talent. I also am convinced that one will have the greatest growth and opportunity in the areas of greatest talent.

The above conclusions enable me to mobilize and utilize their talents. It also puts the employee into the spotlight to demonstrate his or her own unique capabilities.

Team Meetings

The HR leadership team meets every two weeks, with those in remote locations participating via conference call. There are also two global off-site meetings with the HR leadership team: one in the spring and one in the fall. Quarterly meetings are held for all HR employees.

I rarely facilitate meetings. Facilitation is rotated among the staff. Everyone shares and participates. Each submits agenda items prior to the meeting.

We usually focus on current HR and business issues. A business update is always given. Actions are taken to resolve issues, and follow-up is done at the next meeting. Scorecard items are reviewed quarterly.

Working Relationships

I am extremely proud to have a very competent and engaged staff. My skills bring them together to focus and leverage off of each other. I am available twenty-four/seven. I speak to each of them each week for actions, updates, or requests. Every two weeks, I have one-on-one meetings with them or conference calls if they are in remote locations. These are very friendly and informal relationships where people have a comfort level to express any ideas or opinions they may have.

I look for these relationships to be consultative and proactive. This is especially true in the learning organization, with my business partners, and in the compensation and benefits areas. Within this, it is imperative to be innovative and to design best-in-class programs while delivering services to our internal customers. In addition, these relationships should include being able to understand the business and how to support it from an HR perspective, while driving business decisions and taking into consideration the implications on people.

The Relationship with, Role of, and Participation of Our President in HR Meetings

After working four years with Angel Ruiz, president of Market Unit North America for Ericsson, I can say he genuinely understands HR. He understands the strategic value of the workforce, the costs of the human capital, and the demands for increasing revenue, which can only be realized through the workforce. He is a strong supporter and ally of the HR function in general. He casts the shadow of a leader who is a role model for our values, principles, and operational excellence. We like to work with him, and he inspires us to do our best. In addition, he realizes that the HR function is critical to executing our strategic plan and achieving our company's goals. Angel also understands that, if we are an employer of choice, we can exceed growth and profitability by attracting the best talent.

Angel is a very friendly and compassionate executive. He is very extroverted and always takes the human and business aspects into consideration when making a decision. We have an excellent working relationship built on mutual trust. He says what he means, and he means what he says. There are no hidden agendas. Since his office is ten feet away from mine, communication is constant.

Ensure that the Vision Reaches Key Players

We are a company with simple and consistent messages. All employees hear these messages in their meetings as communicated through the HR business partners. The HR staff hears these messages in my meetings, and they have heard them personally from the Swedish senior vice president of HR, Marita Hellberg. Ericsson also uses short message service (SMS) to our phones to deliver critical messages, e-mails, and general meeting Webcasts.

To motivate employees, you should:

1. Always be visible, accessible, and approachable
2. Reward, acknowledge, and celebrate achievement
3. Offer opportunities for employees to improve (e.g., projects, training)
4. Thank employees for contributions—either personally or via e-mail
5. Schedule fun activities to generate energy
6. Invite employees to lunch or breakfast
7. Coach and mentor
8. Be flexible and empathetic when personal issues arise
9. Use reward programs including gift certificates and tickets to sporting events

In summary, there is no substitution for the human touch to motivate people. Take your time and show a true interest in your employees' professional and personal endeavors. Many times, this may mean more to them than receiving a gift or money from your company's reward programs.

Jill Little is vice president of human resources and organization for Ericsson Americas, which includes all of the Ericsson businesses in North America, Central America, South America, and the Caribbean. A five-year employee of Ericsson, she previously served the company as vice president of people and culture for Latin America. She was appointed to her current position in July of 2001.

Prior to joining Ericsson, she served in a number of positions of increasing responsibility in the human resources career field on an international basis, concentrating on the United States and Latin America.

Some of Ms. Little's various international assignments included America Online, Coca Cola, Bristol-Myers Squibb, Citibank, and Chiquita Conglomerate. Throughout her career, she has lived in the United States, Central America, Europe, the Caribbean, and South America. Fluent in English and Spanish, she also has a working knowledge of German.

Ms. Little holds a B.S. in foreign service from Georgetown University and an M.A. in international management from the American Graduate School of International Management. She is a member of the advisory council for the School of Management at the University of Texas at Dallas and serves on the board of directors for the Juvenile Diabetes Research Foundation's greater Dallas chapter.

Dedication: *This chapter is dedicated to Marita Hellberg, senior vice president of human resources and organization at L.M. Ericsson; Angel Ruiz, president of Market Unit North America for Ericsson Inc.; my world-class human resources team; and my dedicated assistant, Cerella Long.*

The opinions expressed in this chapter are those of the author, and do not necessarily represent the position of Ericsson or other individuals identified herein.

Managing HR for Results

Craig R. Gill

Former Senior Vice President in Charge of
Human Resources

New York Life Insurance Co.

A Look at My Management Style

There are three elements that characterize my management style. One is that I believe in the power of shared goals in a shared context. I have found that most people possessing a minimum level of passion and capability for something will do the right thing if they are clear on what the right thing is. Often in corporations, and particularly in human resources (HR) departments, which tend to be more reactive than proactive, people are not aligned around a set of shared goals and priorities.

Secondly, I believe in bringing people with a diversity of opinions and backgrounds to debate how goals may best be achieved, and then reaching a decision and moving forward in unison. I tend to do things that are transformational, which first requires creating a context so people can understand the gaps between what they have been delivering and what is required to meet business goals. This process of examining gaps can be motivational for some people and very threatening for others. I work closely with those who are threatened by what is required in the future organization and lead them to make a choice. Ultimately, each member of the team has to accept the need for change and make a commitment to the goals of the organization, or leave the team.

Third, I believe a team gains energy and confidence by measuring and communicating results. This can be a daunting task for some HR people who have seldom been evaluated on quantitative measures. However, measurement of effectiveness in achieving business impacts may be the key thing that helps transform a poorly regarded HR function into one that is acknowledged as valuable to the business.

At the end of the day, I maintain that the purpose of HR is to deliver five things (see figure below). Three of these things are highly aligned with the strategy of the enterprise, including a complementary human capital strategy or "people strategy" that details what is required of the workforce in terms of skills, performance levels, and expense; the flow of talent through the organization in terms of hiring, promotions, and exits; and a working environment that is attractive, motivational, and supports teamwork. The other two HR deliverables are more generic (and, as a result, are increasingly being outsourced to third parties). These include the delivery of core HR services such as payroll, at costs that are competitive, and adherence to compliance and control activities required by law.

What is HR in business to deliver?

HR is accountable for delivering value to the enterprise in five key areas, bounded by four often-competing market demands

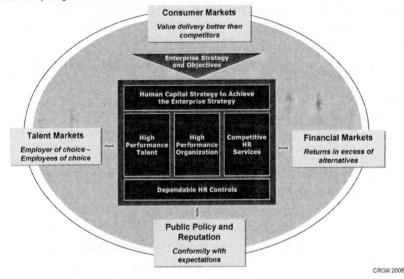

CRGill 2006

The challenge for HR is that it's not easy to achieve results consistently in all five areas. The market forces affecting the enterprise are dynamic and continually shifting. For instance, during the recent recession, many companies had to cut costs, including HR budgets, in order to meet profit targets. However, with higher unemployment, it was relatively easier to hire and retain talented workers, so HR programs were less important. With a return to tighter labor markets, HR is being challenged to deliver better hiring and retention, but to also keep budgets lean. So my vision for managing the HR team is ultimately to operate as a leadership team of a "business inside a business"—setting goals, making decisions, executing, and measuring the results of how HR affects the success of the larger enterprise.

Successful Personality Traits

A successful HR professional must possess a seriousness of purpose around his or her role and impact on the business and workforce. For example, a head of benefits I have worked with—I'll call her Mary—is a great example. Mary thinks from the business standpoint and is financially astute; however, she also understands how her programs and decisions affect everyday people. We put in place a new consumer-directed health care plan, and Mary was great at working both sides of the issue. In fact, she was so adept at catering to both the financial and human aspects that senior management almost considered her an ardent socialist for her stance in pricing health care options, while HR people viewed her as an extreme capitalist for her steadfast focus on bottom-line savings!

Ultimately, intelligence, accountability, and persistence are characteristics I look for in team members. Trying different ways to get to the goal and being willing to deal with the setbacks other business executives experience in pursuing ever-escalating requirements for results is key. I also have found that successful HR professionals have to demonstrate an artful balance between being supportive of people while also stepping up and confronting problems and inappropriate behaviors—especially when the behaviors come from senior managers. Successful HR requires courage grounded in commitment to the long-term success of the business.

Setting Goals for the Team

Using a recent example in which the senior HR team of a Fortune 100 multinational company set out to create a system of shared goals, we started first from the business strategy. The business at the time was in a turnaround situation. Money was tight, and expenses had to be cut sharply. At the same time, we needed to retain and motivate talented individuals to stay and deliver new products and services.

The HR leadership team met over several sessions to develop a highly focused set of goals and measures for the year, including a 50 percent budget cut for HR and some key leadership development goals. These goals were tested with the chief executive officer and senior management, refined, and then formed the "contract" between HR and the business for the year. Each person in HR set performance goals for the year to specifically support one or more of the HR "contracts."

In another example, I was leading an HR team that was given the goal to transform its operations by cutting administrative costs while improving programs to aid in business growth. The HR team was stuck—they could not see how they could each accomplish the many priorities within their different groups and the work of the transformation. We went through a process of identifying those priorities that were truly unique to one group and those for which we were dependent upon one another. These were distilled out to determine which areas were linked and which areas intertwined with each other. There were a few that one organization could do itself. I dealt with them in terms of one-on-one goal cascade; however, the rest realized that there were shared goals. We then laid them out and cascaded individual goals attached to that. This then became the agenda for our weekly leadership team meetings, where we monitored our shared goals as well as what we were doing and what roadblocks stood in the way of accomplishing our objectives.

Debating and Deciding

HR faces some tough challenges, and too often there is a tendency to substitute discussion for action. I believe it is the role of the head of HR, as a member of the senior management of the business, to set the key requirements for the function. Then it is the role of the senior HR management team to crystallize those requirements into specific objectives. In doing this, it is essential to include the diversity of opinion and experience represented by the team. Some people will bring important perspectives around the rising cost of the workforce and the need to increase productivity, while others will bring practical issues regarding the limitations of HR systems and processes in supporting more programs with less investment.

However, to be productive, the debate must be focused, and then a decision has to be made. One of the chief barriers comes when a new direction requires a change in the organization, and shifting resources. Unfortunately, on more than one occasion I have had to ultimately replace a competent senior HR person when he or she would not put aside the desire to keep his or her work group unchanged, or when he or she would attempt to subvert the new direction.

Measuring Success

There has to be a measurement or a condition of satisfaction for each goal to turn into action and results. In the earlier example of the company in turnaround, we did two very important things that turned a set of important goals into actions aligned across the whole of HR, and some stunning results.

First, as described above, the HR leadership team created a "contract" around several goals that were key to the success of the business. Second—and this is what made the biggest difference—we made a commitment to the senior management of the business that we would come back to them after six months and review our progress. We set about starting to track certain aspects and then created a status report at six months and sat down formally one on one with senior management. They were surprised that we came back to show where we stood and were more surprised to see some great results. In some cases, we were off track; however, we described what we were doing to correct things. At the end of the year, we pulled together a concise, seven-chart presentation that showed what we set out to do with each goal and the results. By doing these things, we achieved better quantitative and qualitative results than we had the year before, cut HR costs by more than 50 percent, and the top thirty officers in the business gave us a solid "B" average on our report card in terms of the value HR had added to the business.

HR Today Versus HR Five Years Ago

The three things that have changed most over the years are the pervasiveness of outsourcing, the use of data in measuring and managing HR programs, and the growing appreciation for certain HR disciplines by senior business executives. There has been so much outsourcing of the daily functions that HR work is just being done better in general. Of course, we do not get any extra points for delivering the paychecks accurately and on time or answering the benefits questions well. People expect you to do that. However, most HR departments do not receive as many knocks from management for making mistakes because they have outsourced the basic functions.

In terms of HR data and measures, while there is still a long way to go in many organizations, by and large I see people regularly measuring key processes. This is partly due to better availability of useful data from HR systems such as PeopleSoft and SAP and partly a result of management's insistence that HR demonstrate its value. Five years ago, the focus was on cutting costs during a recession—and as a result, there was much focus on benchmarking and reducing transactional costs, largely through outsourcing. Now, senior management is increasingly interested in how HR is helping to attract and develop skilled workers and especially how the cadre of leaders is being developed to drive business growth and ensure succession.

Common Stumbling Blocks

While there are a number of people in HR roles who are highly valued, until recently HR has not been a place to attract a lot of high-quality talent. I think the number-one restraining force of HR being what it really needs to be is that there is an insufficient level of talent in the function. And looking forward, I am concerned that there are not enough top people coming into the function.

The basic premise of HR transformation and outsourcing activities has been that once administrative processes are automated and outsourced, then HR people can have the time to focus on "value-added work," including talent management and organizational effectiveness. Unfortunately, many HR organizations seem to get stuck in fully making the transition, continuing to get involved in transactions and leaving the business leaders to use external consultants to accomplish organizational and talent goals. The simple fact in many such cases is that the HR people who remain after outsourcing have neither the skills nor the experience to diagnose and solve business-related problems and act as professional, in-house consultants. And fewer still have the training and temperament for the types of quantitative analysis and decision support that characterize leading HR operations. Clearly, more has to be done in attracting skilled people into the profession.

Craig R. Gill brings the perspective and experience of a business executive to his work in leading the transformation of human resource departments both as a human resources executive and senior consulting advisor. His areas of expertise include executing large-scale reengineering and change initiatives, integrating performance and talent management strategies, and developing leaders. He is passionate about expanding the impacts and productivity of individuals and organizations and in delivering measurable returns on investments in human capital. Most recently, he served as senior vice president in charge of human resources for the New York Life Insurance Company, a major financial services firm. In that role, he led a significant transformation of human resources, including reorganization, automation, and outsourcing of core human resources services, and introduction of new strategies for performance management, diversity, and consumer-directed health care, which will reduce spending by over $40 million.

Prior to New York Life, Mr. Gill was a senior executive with Deloitte, one of the world's largest professional services firms, where he led the Northeast U.S. human capital practice that helps businesses attract and retain a competitive workforce, increase the productivity of their organizations, and achieve excellence in their human resources functions. His Fortune 500 clients included a global pharmaceutical company, a leader in children's publishing, and a manufacturing conglomerate.

Prior to joining Deloitte, Mr. Gill led corporate-wide leadership development and organizational effectiveness for Lucent Technologies, a $10 billion global communications networking company. Among his accomplishments, he broke down organizational barriers and reduced executive staffing costs through the design and execution of new leadership succession programs. He started up and ran Lucent's intensive senior leadership development program, which was cited as a best practice by the National Center on Education and the Economy. He worked with management teams in the United States, Asia, and Europe to accelerate product cycle times and growth rates as part of an enterprise-wide culture change initiative. Additionally, he led the effort to fundamentally transform Lucent's human resources operations, which resulted in cost reductions of more than 50 percent, while measurably improving operations and gaining strong support from business leaders.

A native of Washington, D.C., Mr. Gill received his undergraduate degree from Bucknell University and completed the executive program at Dartmouth University's Amos Tuck School. After an early career in consumer finance, he joined AT&T Corporation, rapidly advancing to the position of account executive and industry consultant and achieving top sales honors in the launch of AT&T's new computer product line. For four years, he was the New England area general manager responsible for communication systems sales to more than 50,000 of AT&T's small business customers. During that time, his operation was among the top 10 percent of offices in new account growth, while leading the country in employee satisfaction. As national sales operations director, he was responsible for U.S. incentive compensation and sales force productivity and led the initiative that reduced turnover by 40 percent through innovative sales management practices.

Moving from line management to the field of human resources, Mr. Gill joined AT&T's multimedia products group as human resources director. The next year, he led the human resources policy and operations work required to divide 300,000 employees among three companies as part of a record-setting divestiture. He then joined Lucent Technologies as human resources vice president, responsible for supporting Lucent's corporate staff organizations. To quickly launch Lucent's new data networking business unit, he was asked to lead all start-up human resources activities, which included staffing a new executive team and sales force as well as introducing an entirely new compensation and benefits structure.

Mr. Gill lives in New Jersey with his wife, Denise, and his son, Jonathan. He is active in sports, community, and professional organizations.

***Acknowledgment:** Special thanks to Dave Ulrich, who taught me the value of "human resource deliverables," and to the many human resources professionals with whom I have been privileged to work over the years, who taught me the value of keeping the "human" in human resources.*